The Magic of Bewitched Trivia

The Magic of Bewitched Trivia

by Gina Meyers

iUniverse, Inc.
New York Lincoln Shanghai

The Magic of Bewitched Trivia

Copyright © 2007 by Gina Marie Meyers

All rights reserved. No part of this book may be used or reproduced by any means, graphic, electronic, or mechanical, including photocopying, recording, taping or by any information storage retrieval system without the written permission of the publisher except in the case of brief quotations embodied in critical articles and reviews.

iUniverse books may be ordered through booksellers or by contacting:

iUniverse
2021 Pine Lake Road, Suite 100
Lincoln, NE 68512
www.iuniverse.com
1-800-Authors (1-800-288-4677)

Because of the dynamic nature of the Internet, any Web addresses or links contained in this book may have changed since publication and may no longer be valid.

The views expressed in this work are solely those of the author and do not necessarily reflect the views of the publisher, and the publisher hereby disclaims any responsibility for them.

Unless otherwise noted, all photos courtesy of the Gina and David Lawrence Meyers collection, Mark Simpson collections, and Lori Kearney professional photography.

ISBN: 978-0-595-44744-2 (pbk)
ISBN: 978-0-595-89065-1 (ebk)

Printed in the United States of America

Do not just settle for anything, reach for the stars!
To the Glowing People in my life: David, Makenna, Lauren, and Lucas.

Pictured from top left to top right, The Meyers family in the Big Apple, David, Gina, and Makenna Meyers. From bottom left to right, Lucas and Lauren Meyers. The Meyers family is hopeful that the next Broadway musical they will see will be *Bewitched* on Broadway!

Pictured from left to right: Kasey Rogers, *Bewitched's* consummate actress, Louise Tate #2, "the boss's wife", and the author of *The Magic of Bewitched Trivia and More*, and *The Magic of Bewitched Trivia* book Gina Meyers.
Photo credit: David Lawrence Meyers (June 2005)

The crew from Fanatical filming a sequence for the television episode in which my *Bewitched* fandom is shown. The photos are of the Bewitched Bash from the Summer of 2006. Photo courtesy of Lori Kearney Photography. Gina Meyers engaged in conversation with Rick Bentley, television and movie critic.

Gina Meyers and Fanatical Crew filming the significance of the framed photo of Gina in a yellow Volkswagen convertible bug. Gina is describing how in the 1970's spin-off *Tabitha*, Lisa Hartman drove a yellow convertible bug, and coincidentally enough so did Nicole Kidman in the 2005 movie adaptation of *Bewitched*.

David Meyers and the Fanatical Film Crew in the Meyers' kitchen.

Bewitched Fans enjoying the ambience of a Bewitching Evening as preparing for the charity auction.
Pictured from left to right are Carly, Johnna, and Greg Overin. On far right is Alan Hill, authors' dad.

THE MAGIC OF *BEWITCHED* TRIVIA
TABLE OF CONTENTS

101 Things You Always Wanted to Know About Bewitched xviii
The Bewitched Theme Song Lyrics xxiv
How Well Do You Know The Stephens? xxv
Acknowledgments xxvii
Introduction xxxiii

1	With A Twitch of The Nose, It's Magic!	1
2	Seeing Double, The Two Darrin's	15
3	Character Traits	21
4	Supernatural Situation Comedy	44
	The Cast of Bewitched	44
	Occasional Roles	45
	Bewitched Technical Credits	45
	The Bewitched Movie Cast Credits	48
	Ratings	50
	The Emmys	53
	Bewitching Remakes & Semi-Remakes	57
	I Dream of Jeannie Similar Storyline	59
	Shows Dick York Missed	59
	Regulars Only	60
	TV & Film Credits	62
	Bewitched Episodes	73
5	Cosmic Connection	144

xi

6	Mangled Monikers	153
	Darrin Name Quiz	*153*
	Unearthly Terminology	*154*
	Famous Last Words	*156*
7	Totally Trivia	159
	Ultimate Bewitched Episode Trivia Challenge	*160*
	It's All Relative	*173*
	Wives	*175*
	Cosmic Characteristics	*176*
	Which Witch Is Which?	*177*
	Who Said It?	*179*
	The Bewitched Puzzle	*180*
	Bewitched Stars	*181*
	The Bewitching Hour Questions	*182*
	His or Hers?	*186*
	Easy Multiple Choice	*187*
	Tabitha Comedy Trivia	*193*
	I Dream of Jeannie Déjà vu Trivia Questions	*195*
	Tabitha Stephens Trivia	*196*
	Romancing Taking Flight, Samantha and Darrin Trivia	*198*
	Witches and Warlocks are my Favorite Things Trivia	*201*
	Extreme Home Makeover Trivia	*203*
	Answers	*206*
8	In Witch Conclusion	212
	A little about Me:	*213*
	Want More Information on Bewitched?	*216*
	Causes Worth Supporting	*218*

About the Author 221

Welcome to The Magic Show!

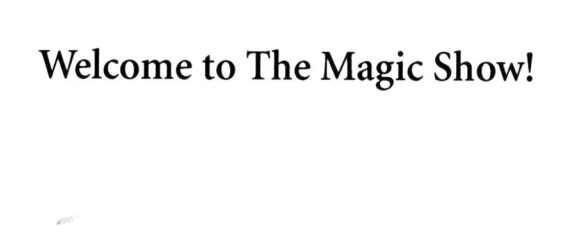

"I love you and I want you to be happy."
—Samantha as said to Darrin in Episode #17,
"*A is For Aardvark*".

Gina Meyers, after the *Bewitched* Bash, posing with *The Magic of Bewitched Trivia and More book* and a *Bewitched* Vintage British book.

xvi

Few television series have *"bewitched"* millions of TV viewers as much as *Bewitched*. This magical series started over forty years ago and still is popular on DVD, TV Land, Nick at Nite, on You Tube, on Video, and all over the globe. *Bewitched* made its way to the big screen in 2005 with megastars Nicole Kidman playing a Samantha type character named Isabel Bigelow and actor/comedian Will Ferrell portraying Darrin. Academy Award winners Shirley McClaine and Michael Caine co-starred in the *Bewitched* movie/television adaptation. McClaine portrayed meddlesome mother-in-law Endora, and Caine played Samantha's proper father, Nigel Bigelow, also known as Maurice. Nora Ephron, director of the hit movie *Sleepless in Seattle,* was at the helm of directing as well as writing the *Bewitched* movie. Nora's sister Delia also contributed to the writing of the *Bewitched* screenplay.

Bewitched blends reality and fantasy. The show and characters have become an endearing part of Pop culture history. *Bewitched* continues to gain new fans and enchant them with its' special brand of magic.

Part of the magic is that Samantha demonstrates that witches have problems just like everybody else. *Bewitched* is a mix on the traditional, it is witch—mortal marriage and all of the mayhem that accompanies such a union. Television is a staple and a partial expression of our American culture. Apart from televisions pure entertainment value, it can enrich our lives in a multitude of ways. Television can help erase stigma, combat prejudice, inform us of happenings, and it can help us relate to television characters and learn from them. As Agnes Moorehead so aptly put it, "*Bewitched* is distorted from reality, and nothing is as dull as constant reality."

In our culture, appearance is almost as important as skill and ability. Sometimes in certain circumstances, and professions/vocations, beauty is more important than knowledge. Even though the majority of the cast and crew lived in the glare of Hollywood lights and the glimmer of Tinsel Town, Elizabeth Montgomery remained true to herself and her values. Where plastic surgery was the norm and in 2007 still is commonplace in Hollywood, Elizabeth Montgomery never bobbed her turned-up nose nor capped her two upper front teeth, which were crooked. As she put it, "It's my snaggletooth in front, all witches have one and I don't think it is worth going to a dentist and spending hundreds of dollars to repair it. You couldn't cap just that one, you'd have to do them all and then you'd end up with a mouth full of Chiclets." Hollywood seems to agree with Elizabeth Montgomery's philosophy and will pay homage to the actress approximately twelve years after her passing. In January of 2008, Elizabeth Montgomery will receive a star on the Hollywood Walk of Fame! A permanent memento and fixture that immortalizes a woman whose shelf life will never expire!

101 Things You Always Wanted to Know About Bewitched

Trivia Tidbit:
The original actress that ABC had chosen, was Tammy Grimes. She turned down ABC's offer, and instead opted for another script that became The Tammy Grimes Show. The Tammy Grimes Show, was showcased in 1966. Tammy played a character named Tamantha, which sounds a lot like Samantha, minus the S, with a T in its' place. Tammy's co-star was Dick Sargent and Maudie Prickett was a featured regular (She played as Tabitha's teacher). The series unfortunately was not well received and it lasted only four weeks.

1. The original script title for *Bewitched* was *The Witches of Westport*.
2. *Bewitched* was a Screen Gems Production.
3. The original pilot script had the main character names as Darrin and Cassandra Douglas.
4. Elizabeth Montgomery was married to *Bewitched*'s director, William Asher.
5. 306 episodes of *Bewitched* were filmed, however, only 254 aired.
6. The first 74 episodes of *Bewitched* were filmed in Black and White.
7. William Asher and Elizabeth Montgomery created a production company entitled, Ashmont Productions.
8. Ashmont Productions was a combination of Mr. Asher and Ms. Montgomery's two last names, quite similar to the technique initially utilized by Lucille Ball and Desi Arnez with Desilu Productions, which was a blending of their respective names.
9. The first *Bewitched* filmed in color was Episode #75, "Nobody's Perfect".
10. Episode #74, "Prodigy", was the last black-and-white *Bewitched* episode that appeared on network television. It aired on June 9, 1966. It was also the last show where Alice Pearce played the role of Gladys Kravitz, "The World's Nosiest Neighbor".
11. Towards the end of the second season, unfortunately, Alice Pearce passed away due to complications from ovarian cancer and was replaced by veteran actress Sandra Gould.
12. George Tobias exclusively played oblivious neighbor Abner Kravitz for the eight-year span of *Bewitched*. His sister Harriet Kravitz, played by

Mary Grace Canfield appeared on *Bewitched* during the transition time from Alice Pearce to Sandra Gould.

13. Two actors shared the role of Frank Stephens, Darrin's father. Robert F. Simon appeared in six episodes; Roy Roberts appeared in seven episodes.
14. Prior to *Bewitched*, among some of Mr. Asher's' directorial achievements, he worked on the *I Love Lucy Show*, as well as *The Danny Thomas Show*.
15. William Asher and Elizabeth Montgomery married on October 26, 1963. They met on the set of the movie *Johnny Cool*. William Asher was producing and directing and Elizabeth Montgomery was acting in *Johnny Cool*. After their marriage, they sought a project to work on together, the project they chose was *Bewitched*. The first few episodes had to be filmed around Elizabeth's pregnancy. She was pregnant with their first son, William Allen Asher.
16. Elizabeth Montgomery reported to work exactly three weeks after giving birth to her son William Allen Asher, nicknamed Willy.
17. William Allen Asher has no television counterpart.
18. William Asher and Elizabeth Montgomery produced three offspring, two sons and one daughter.
19. Elizabeth Montgomery's favorite episode was written by a tenth grade English class at Thomas Jefferson High School. It is Episode #213, "Sisters at Heart".
20. "Sisters at Heart" was an episode that dealt with racial prejudice. Tabitha and her friend Lisa, who is African American, desperately want to look alike and become real sisters. Tabitha tries to make herself and Lisa look more alike, but accidentally zaps up black polka dots on herself and white dots on her friend Lisa.
21. Many actors and actresses got their start on *Bewitched*. Rachel Welch as well as Richard Dreyfus are just two stars who premiered on *Bewitched*.
22. Professional Baseball player Willie Mays appeared in Episode #81, "Twitch or Treat". Samantha assures Darrin that Willie is a warlock.
23. Samantha tells Darrin that he is going to be a daddy in Episode #37, "Alias Darrin Stephens".
24. In the fifth season of the show, allegedly, Elizabeth Montgomery was ready to move on to other projects.
25. Elizabeth Montgomery and William Asher were given too sweet a deal to pass on in the show's 5th season, all creative control, and 50% of *Bewitched*'s profits.

26. Elizabeth Montgomery enjoyed playing Samantha's hippy groovy cousin alter ego named Serena.
27. The name credited for Elizabeth Montgomery's portrayal of Serena was Pandora Spocks.
28. Pandora Spocks was a play on words from the Greek mythology story about Pandora's Box.
29. In real life, Elizabeth had a cousin named Panda, nickname for Pandora. She used to be mischievous and would get Elizabeth into trouble as children.
30. Elizabeth Montgomery is the daughter of famous actor Robert Montgomery.
31. Elizabeth Montgomery was born on April 15, 1933.
32. Elizabeth Montgomery passed away on May 18, 1995.
33. Elizabeth Montgomery gave birth to a son that they named Robert Asher. His television counterpart is Tabitha Stephens.
34. Tabitha was initially spelled as Tabatha, and was later changed to Tabitha. The spin-off of *Bewitched* was spelled with an "I" for the brief television series starring Lisa Hartman. Though the pilot episode, starring Liberty Williams dabbled with spelling it "Tabatha".
35. In 1969, Elizabeth gave birth to a daughter that she and her husband named Rebecca Asher. Her television counterpart is Adam Stephens.
36. *Bewitched* was an instant hit! In its' first year, Bewitched was #2 in the Nielson Ratings.
37. Dick Sargent was initially approached to play the part of Darrin Stephens; he however was under contractual obligations to another project.
38. Tammy Grimes, the English stage actress also was approached to participate in *Bewitched*. She turned it down, in favor of another television sitcom, "The Tammy Grimes Show".
39. Along with Tammy Grimes, Dick Sargent also appeared on the "*Tammy Grimes Show*".
40. Dick York suffered from a debilitating spine disorder that was a result of an injury, which he suffered from a movie stunt on the 1959 western, *The Came to Condura*.
41. Dick York, due to his back pain, was not always reliable. Often times, the director and producer would have to change the script at the last minute, to accommodate "the missing Darrin." Please see section **Shows Dick York Missed** for a complete listing.

42. The Asher's did not want to replace Dick York, but the network insisted.
43. The Asher's approached Robert Montgomery concerning playing Samantha's father, unfortunately, he never was on *Bewitched*.
44. Maurice Evans played the role of Maurice, Samantha's warlock father.
45. Maurice had a penchant for reciting Shakespearian soliquies.
46. The Stephens lived at 1164 Morning Glory Circle in Westport, Connecticut.
47. Tabitha is born on telecast January 13, 1966 in Episode #54, "*And Then There Were Three*".
48. Darrin mistakes Serena for his newborn daughter grow-up in "*And Then There Were Three*".
49. Episode #54 is Serena's first appearance.
50. Eve Arden, from the show, "*Our Miss Brooks*" plays the nurse in "*And Then There Were Three*".
51. The *Bewitched* Theme Song Lyrics were written, but never used.
52. The Bewitched Theme Song was written by Jack Keller and Howard Greenfield.
53. *Bewitched* was on ABC networks.
54. *I Dream of Jeannie* was NBC's clone of ABC's *Bewitched*.
55. In June of 1970, Bewitched filmed on location in Salem, Massachusetts. "Bewitched Day" was officially recognized on October the 8th, 1970, by the Mayor of Salem.
56. In June of 2005, TV Land unveiled a 9-foot bronze statue of Samantha that is erected in Lapin Park, which is located in Salem, Massachusetts.
57. Jane Connell played Hephzibah, the high priestess of witches in "*To go or not to Go, That is The Question*".
58. Darrin's ancestor is Darrin the Bold.
59. In the final season of the show (8th), the *Bewitched* cast and crew filmed on location in Europe.
60. An honor bestowed upon Samantha during the series is when she is asked to be "Queen of the Witches".
61. Ruth McDevitt played the old-witch queen in Episode #108, "*Long Live the Queen*".
62. Aunt Clara was played by Marion Lorne.
63. California law required that child actors could only work limited hours, hence the reason for the use of twins on *Bewitched*.
64. Samantha's birthday is June 6th.

65. Aunt Clara was an aging, bumbling witch.
66. Aunt Clara was Samantha's favorite aunt.
67. Darrin's Aunt Marge thought she was a lighthouse.
68. Dick Albain did many of the show's special effects.
69. Larry and Louise Tate's son is named Jonathan.
70. Nancy Kovack played Darrin's ex-fiancée, Sheila Summers.
71. Jack Cassidy played Rance Butler in "*Samantha Goes South for a Spell*."
72. Serena convinces Tommy Boyce and Bobby Hart to sing her song, "I'll Blow You a Kiss in the Wind".
73. Samantha's slogan for Tinkerbelle Diapers is, "Switch to Tinkerbelle Diapers, It is Time for a Change."
74. In Episode #152, "*Weep No More, My Willow*", Dr. Bombay accidentally places a spell on Samantha that makes her weep uncontrollably.
75. Paul Lynde, Who plays Uncle Arthur only appeared in 10 episodes.
76. Endora is allergic to Macedonian dodo birds.
77. Gladys Kravitz often asks to borrow things from Samantha.
78. One time, Abner and Gladys have a fight, and Abner moves in with Darrin and Samantha. Gladys too moves in temporarily with the Stephens.
79. During the span of the series, Endora actually does get Darrin's name correct, a few times at least.
80. Agnes Moorehead appeared in the movie *Citizen Kane*.
81. Uncle Arthur's pet name for Samantha is Sammy.
82. Endora and Arthur are brother and sister.
83. Endora and Maurice have what is termed an informal marriage, though Endora shows no signs of infidelity or wanting a divorce.
84. Maurice often calls Darrin by the name of Dobbin.
85. Darrin's mother Phyllis often has "sick headaches".
86. Darrin's dad, Frank, is interested in get rich quick schemes.
87. Esmeralda, brought into the cast of characters, after Aunt Clara, is a shy witch maid.
88. Samantha's aunts included: Aunt Hagatha, Aunt Clara, and Aunt Enchantra.
89. Dick Sargent became Darrin in the show's sixth season.
90. Imogene Coca played Mary, the Good Fairy in Episode #215 and #216.

91. Dick Sargent became a father in just four episodes with the birth of Adam, in Episode #175, "*And Something Makes Four*".
92. There were 5 Halloween Episodes on *Bewitched*.
93. Mr. Howard McMann, Larry Tate's partner was only shown twice on the series.
94. Darrin was fired 19 times on *Bewitched* by Larry.
95. Darrin quit from McMann & Tate twice.
96. *Bewitched* only won three Emmy Awards.
97. *Bewitched* officially ended on July 1, 1972.
98. *Bewitched* is the only sitcom where a daughter got her own TV spin-off, "Tabitha".
99. Samantha tells Darrin on their wedding night that she is a witch. From the premier episode, "I, Darrin, Take This Witch, Samantha".
100. Dick York missed fourteen shows due to a back injury.
101. Dick York acted in 156 *Bewitched* Episodes, Dick Sargent 84 Episodes.

THE *BEWITCHED* THEME SONG LYRICS

Words and music by Howard Greenfield and Jack Keller

Bewitched, Bewitched, you've got me in your spell.
Bewitched, Bewitched, you know your craft so well.
Before I knew what you were doing, I looked in your eyes.
That brand of woo that you've been brew-in' took me by surprise.

You witch, you witch, one thing is for sure—
That stuff you pitch—just hasn't got a cure.
My heart was under lock and key—but somehow it got unhitched.
I never thought my heart could be had.
But now I'm caught and I'm kinda glad to be—
Bewitched. Bewitched—witched.

*Note: Lyrics never used for *Bewitched*'s opening or closing credits.

How Well Do You Know The Stephens?

1. Samantha does magic by:
   a. Tugging her ear
   b. Blinking her eyes
   c. Wiggling her nose
   d. Crossing her arms

2. Serena's pet name for Larry Tate is.
   a. Peter Cotton Top
   b. Cotton Ball
   c. Peter Rabbit

3. What does Maurice usually call Darrin?
   a. Dobbin
   b. Durweed
   c. Durwood
   d. What's your name

4. What is Darrin Stephens' profession?
   a. He is a professional golfer
   b. He is an astronaut;
   c. He is an advertising executive
   d. He is a marketing director

5. What is the Stephens address?
   a. 1020 Palm Drive
   b. 1164 Morning Glory Circle;
   c. 1313 Mockingbird Lane
   d. 333 Elmwood Drive

How many did you get correct?
0 "Weeell," I think you had better invest in the Bewitched on DVD Collection, to catch up on your deprived childhood.
1 "Hey, not bad."-Serena
2 You probably had difficulty distinguishing between Bewitched and *I Dream of Jeannie*.
3 You have written to at least one of the cast members, or have seriously contemplated doing so.
4 You have named at least one of your pets or a family member after one of the characters from *Bewitched*.
5 "Like wow, totally groovy!" Mr. and Mrs. Stephens would be very proud. Questions1 & 3 though may upset Mr. Stephens.

Answers:
1. c.
2. a.
3. a.
4. c.
5. b.

Acknowledgments

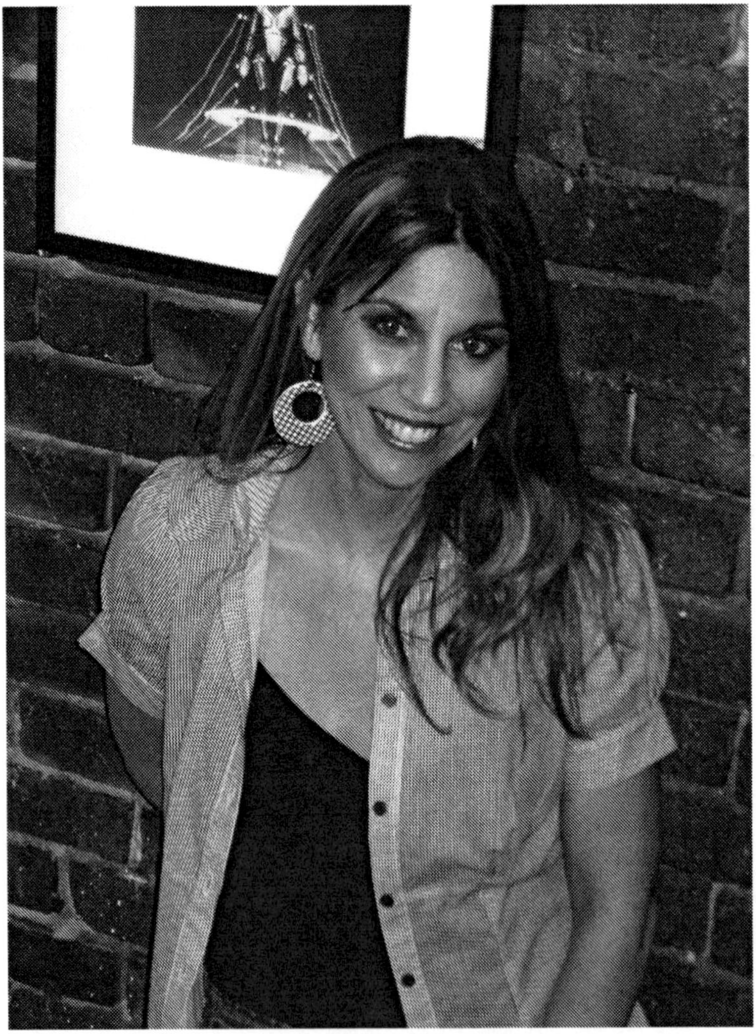

A book is never the work of just one person, or so I've found to be the case in my life. Without the love and support of my other half, David, nothing would ever get accomplished! What a fantastic television show ride we've had with *Bewitched* over the past few years. My dreams could have never prepared me for the real in living color experiences I've had riding the *Bewitched* broom. First off, to think that *Bewitched* would be made into a movie and for it to finally happen, wow! Then to be asked by the media to talk about the movie at a prescreening and on the same weekend to be invited to the "Ranch", a.k.a. the Bewitched façade (shot at the Warner Brothers Studio lot), simply fantabulous!

2005 was full of completely Bewitching moments. In the summer of 2005, while at the Warner Brothers Lot, I met fans of the television sitcom from as far away as Australia. My family got bigger that day! Seeing Kasey Rogers and her longtime love Mark Wood and getting to take photos with them was a huge delight. But I felt a slight disappointment, of the cringe variety, when they left due to heat exhaustion. Most of the fans received a lovely 8x10 glossy photo of Louise and Larry Tate. But, I received a much larger gift that day. Feeling hungry, my husband and I decided to eat at the only decent looking restaurant close to the Ranch, I think it was called Daltons. There was a sign on the door saying it was going to close for good (something about a lease not being renewed), but we decided to go in nevertheless. There in the desolated restaurant seated to our far left were Kasey and Mark. No coincidence. I know a God moment when it happens. Mark excitedly got up and congratulated me on the success of my book. (since Kasey's throat surgery, Mark did a lot of corresponding for Kasey, because it was difficult for her to speak, due to the tracheotomy). I already had a prearranged book signing at the Barnes and Noble in Glendale scheduled for a few weeks later and courageously asked the couple if they were interested in doing a co-book signing event. They agreed and a few weeks later, I had my daughter Lauren to my left and Kasey Rogers to my right for two hours! David took our rambunctious son Lucas on an outing to the local pet store. A young man who was turning fourteen was in the audience. He and his friends came to the book-signing event as his birthday present. He and his friends eagerly asked questions and were doubly surprised that a real cast member was there!

"Oh, my stars!" I found my Darrin, in the Autumn of 1995. He materialized at my work, in the break room, his van broke down on the freeway and he walked to his sisters' workplace (which I worked at too). The metaphysical continuum was definitely supernaturally bringing the two of us together, as only four days earlier, at the tender age of twenty-four, I had sworn off guys all together, using my own incantation something to the effect, "Good stuff like that never happens to me, I think I need a break from guys for awhile!" During a morning McMann & Tate type meeting, a coworker of mine, a Sheila look-alike had told us of her chance encounter at a bar over the weekend, and how she had met the love and of her life, and she was certain that they would marry—and unite in holy matrimony quickly. Maybe she had been bitten by a chi chi fly I thought to myself, and then the incredulously unbelieving cynical part of me came out with the comment, "Nothing Good like that ever happens to me." Why? Because up until that point I truly believed that the only things magical about me was my adolescent fascination with a television show. The moment I let go, was the moment magic happened! My boyfriend at the time, who actually is named Darin, (his mother had named him after you know who), found my transformation magnifying. Suddenly, he wanted to go all over the cosmos with me. But, it was David's persistence and his invitations to such exotic galas as the Galactic Rejuvenation and Dinner Dance that really sealed the deal. Nine months later, we were married.

Thank you to all of my high school teachers and college professors that were instrumental in my development as a writer and as a person. Special thanks to Mr. Jim Jessen who was my history and political science teacher at Oak Grove High School. He also agreed to be the mentor teacher when I started peer counseling. Thank you Mr. Jessen for being a great encouragement to me. Also, to Mr. Jewel, my psychology teacher who gave me an A+ on all of my journals and listened to my philosophical ideas on life. I enjoyed listening to your stories of walking from Los Angeles to San Francisco in the sixties and exposing the class to music from Pink Floyd.

I would like to thank my husband David for all of his love, dedication, support, and belief in the spirit of The *Magic of Bewitched: Trivia and More* book and accompanying books. Thank you Lauren and Makenna for watching countless hours of *Bewitched* with mommy and laughing along! Lucas, there is nothing funnier than hearing you sing over and over again, 'Bewitched … bewitched", and when you say, "there is magic in this". You recently recited this phrase when you helped mommy put a plaque up on the wall from high school.

Thank you Dad for encouraging my interest in *Bewitched* and allowing me to wake up at 5:45a.m., so I could watch the show on cable. Thank you Mom for reading my manuscript, correcting it, and for writing words of encouragement. Grandma Rose, even though you are in heaven now, thanks for reading my manuscript from beginning to end, and for saying, it was "good"! Auntie and Uncle, thank you for placing my spiral bound *Bewitched* recipe book in the front window of your Mount Shasta bookstore. Patrick thanks for not razzing me too much about liking *Bewitched*. Rose, thanks for letting me be Samantha during all those summertime *Bewitched* plays that I put on in my living room when we were kids. If I had to do it again, I would not make you be Serena every time.

To quote Esmeralda, "Best witches" to the hundreds of loyal *Bewitched* fans who have written to me over the past fifteen years and who have shared stories, pictures, and poems. Also, to the subscribers of the Morning Glory Gazette Newsletter (*The local paper is called the Gazette as shown in episodes #34, 105, 138, 152, 183.*)
Magic of *Bewitched* Fan Club
PO Box 26734 Fresno, Ca. 93729.

On a professional note: merci beaucoup husband, David Meyers, for the many years you've logged editing, scanning, discussing ideas for the book, and helping to make the book a reality. Special thanks to David Keil, noted *Bewitched* historian, for sharing information on episodes and series history. Thank you to Cynthia, Oscar, Genie, Rex and others who have hosted Bewitched Booksignings (mainly through Barnes and Noble) and events. TVTropolis and all of the people affiliated with the filming of the Bewitched segment for Fanatical, you rock! Thanks Stephanie Pickering and film crew Bart, Adrien, and sound guy, oops, I can't remember your name. To anyone I have forgotten to mention by name (like the sound guy, graphic designers, editors, publishers, TV producers, toy collectors, professional writers, etc.) that I have crossed paths with in putting this project together, "thank you"!
A special thank you to Mark Simpson for sharing his love of Bewitched with all of us in the form of Bewitched Conventions and photographs. Way to go!!!!!!!!

INTRODUCTION

Bewitched, reminiscent of all great television sitcoms, shows us our place in life. It gives us a glimpse of the family we would like to be a part of, the job we wish to land, the person we would like to become, the friends we would like to have, and the dreams we wish to fulfill. Like a fairy godmother's magic dust, a good sitcom covers reality with fantasy and illusion and provides the modern liberated child in all of us with the security of reruns on the tube.

Bewitched teaches a valuable lesson, that there is "magic" in us and it is waiting to be freed. A talent cannot be suppressed; a gift cannot be ignored in order to please someone else. In Samantha's case, her talent was witchcraft, and she tried to please her mortal husband Darrin by abstaining from her craft.

A gift is irrepressible and eventually it will emerge. Look at all the chaos that occurred when Sam tried to suppress her talent.

Bewitched showed fans that we all have special hidden talents/"magic" that need to be explored.

The Magic of Bewitched: Trivia book is meant to be informational, fun, and a treasure to add to your *Bewitched* collection. You, the reader, are invited to the "magic" show.

We want love to be magical. We want to live simply and happily. No one wants their life to be humdrum, married to an individual that sometimes acts like a dum-dum, live in a home in the middle of doldrums, with average children. We all desire to be special and unique. Not only do we want to meet Mr. or Miss Right, we want it to be a mystical experience. In a life that has countless trying moments, we deserve something magical to cherish. Just go back for a moment in time—look down memory lane. What are your fondest memories? Do they seem unreal, like a dream? That is exactly why *Bewitched* was so appealing. It made us secretly wish that there were real witches like Samantha that turned mundane life into magic!

CHAPTER 1

With A Twitch of The Nose, It's Magic!

Eye of newt and toe of frog, flip the switch, and see her twitch, and watch Bewitched

"The fact that I don't look exotic and witchlike is an enormous boost for the show's form of humor."-Elizabeth Montgomery

Once upon an enchanted spell, there was a winsome witch with a necromantic nose and a flare for mischief, who married a mere mortal named Darrin. They lived in the heart of suburbia at 1164 Morning Glory Circle in Westport, Connecticut. He was an advertising man, she a sexy floor scrubbing, laundry toting, child rearing, house witch. Or as Look Magazine put it, "Samantha is a clean-scrubbed, suburban Everywoman, with her caldron hooked to the rotisserie." (*Look*, 1965) Samantha Stephens had the ability to pop up anything she desired, but what she desired most was a quirky young man by the name of Darrin Stephens. This love story, which lasted for eight seasons, was originally aired from September 17, 1964 to July 1, 1972 on ABC networks as a Screen Gems Production. After each episode, the *Bewitched* audience anticipated what benign witchcraft antics Samantha (and/or relatives) would stir up next.

In the first pilot, "I Darrin, Take This Witch, Samantha," it is revealed that Samantha is a witch. Samantha's mother, Endora, visits her daughter on her wedding night. Regretting that her daughter has married a mortal, Endora becomes determined to break up the marriage. Samantha decides to tell Darrin that he has unknowingly married a witch. To convince him of her powers, Samantha performs a series of tricks. After she has shown him of her extraordinary powers, Darrin makes her promise never to use her witchcraft again. Later in the episode, a former girlfriend of Darrin's, named Sheila, invites the newlyweds over for a dinner party. This is done under the guise that

Sheila wants to congratulate the happy newlyweds. Instead, Sheila makes every effort to humiliate Samantha. After enduring Darrin's ex-girlfriend's insults a number of times, Sam (nickname for Samantha) cannot resist the temptation to embarrass the host by employing the use of witchcraft.

The episodes that follow are a variation of the same theme. Darrin wants Samantha to stop practicing witchcraft and to settle into being a nice suburban homemaker. Samantha, on the other hand, is continually tempted to twitch her nose to clean up the kitchen when unexpected company arrives, to settle a score when she or Darrin is being insulted or embarrassed, or to save an advertising account for Darrin when a client is disgruntled.

The performers on *Bewitched* were impeccably cast in their respective roles. Their characters were flavorful and refreshing. Elizabeth Montgomery portrayed Samantha Stephens, the intelligent and beautiful housewife with a twitch; Dick York (1964-1969) and Dick Sargent (1969-1972) played the role of Darrin Stephens, the Madison Avenue ad man married to a witch. Agnes Moorehead played the egocentric, meddling mother-in-law named Endora; and David White played Darrin's greedy, hypocritical boss named Larry Tate.

Other brilliant performers included Marion Lorne as Aunt Clara, an aging, bumbling witch; Alice Ghostley (played a similar role to that of Marion Lorne's Aunt Clara after Lorne passed away), as Esmeralda, a shy witch maid; Alice Pearce (1964-1966) and Sandra Gould (1966-1972) as the Stephens' infamous nosy neighbor Gladys Kravitz; George Tobias as the passive Abner Kravitz; Irene Vernon (1964-1966) and Kasey Rogers (1966-1972) as Larry Tate's worrisome and sensitive wife, Louise; Paul Lynde (1965-1972) as Uncle Arthur, Samantha's practical joking uncle who was a warlock; Bernard Fox as Samantha's family physician, "the witch doctor"; Maurice Evans played Maurice, Samantha's distinguished and proper father; Robert F. Simon and Roy Roberts sharing the role of Frank Stephens, Darrin's father; and Mabel Albertson as Phyllis Stephens, the easily upset and nerve wracked mother of Darrin.

Twins portrayed both of the Stephen's children. Erin and Diane Murphy (1966-1972) played the role of Tabitha, the little witch daughter of Samantha and Darrin (Erin later resumed the role of Tabitha); and David and Greg Lawrence (1971-1972) portrayed Adam, the Stephen's warlock son.

There were also memorable characters who made recurring guest appearances on the show and they were: Aunt Hagatha, Samantha's aunt, played by Ysabel MacClosky and Reta Shaw (*The Ghost and Mrs. Muir*); Howard McMann, (Larry Tate's partner in the advertising firm, McMann & Tate) portrayed by Leon Ames and Gilbert Roland; Margaret McMann, Howard's wife, played by Louise Sorel; Betty, (Darrin's secretary) played by Marcia Wallace, Samantha Scott, and Jean Blake; the drunk Darrin meets at the bar, played by Dick Wilson; and the Apothecary, (the old warlock flirt) played by Bernie Kopell (*Love Boat*).

"Oh, My Guest Stars"

Besides just having a brilliant cast and crew, *Bewitched* also had a plethora of grand guests. Some were already stars in their own right, others on the brink of stardom.

Several television and screen legends appeared on the show, such as Imogene Coca, Cesar Romero, Peter Lawford, Grace Lee Whitney (*Star Trek*) [played in "It Shouldn't Happen to a Dog," as Babs Livingston], June Lockhart (*Lost In Space*) [portrayed Mrs. Burns in "Little Pitchers have Big Fears"], Adam West (*Batman*) [played a man named Kermit in "Love Is Blind"], Bill Daily (*I Dream of Jeannie*), James Doohan (*Star Trek*) [played Walter Brocken in "A Strange Little Visitor"], Dick Gautier (*When Things Were Rotten*), Richard Bull (*Voyage to the Bottom of the Sea*), Jonathan Harris (*Lost In Space*), Pat Priest (*The Munsters*) and many more.

Rachel Welch and Richard Dreyfuss both made their professional acting debuts on *Bewitched*. Raquel Welch played the stewardess in the episode titled, "*Witch or Wife*," and Richard Dreyfuss (*Close Encounters of the Third Kind*) played Rodney in, "*Man's Best Friend.*"

Many child actors and actresses played parts on *Bewitched*. Childhood star Jimmy Mathers played Marshall Burns in Episode #6, "*Little Pitchers have Big Fears.*" Johnny Whitaker (*Family Affair*) acted in Episode #171, "*Samantha and the Beanstalk.*" Other child actors and actresses included Maureen McCormick (*The Brady Bunch*), Billy Mumy (*Lost In Space*), and Danny Bonaduce (*The Partridge Family*) and a host more of child actors were brought in on occasion.

Bewitched not only cast television regulars, screen legends, and a host of child actors, they also invited famous celebrities to the show. Willie Mays made his television debut as a Warlock in Episode #81, "*Twitch or Treat.*" Los Angeles Rams defensive end Decon Jones played in Episode #171, "*Samantha and the Bean stock,*" (first episode that aired with Dick Sargent as Darrin) he was the guardian of the giant's castle. Also, singers Tommy Boyce and Bobby Hart played themselves in Episode #192, "*Serena Stops the Show.*"

A 1968 *TV Guide* study linked income and education with TV viewing habits, and showed *Bewitched* as #7 among the Top 10 most popular shows of individuals with one or more years of college. Among individuals who had a grade school education, they ranked the show *Family Affair* as #7.

The study was for a 6-week period ending December 3, 1967, and showed that the grade school-educated households' tastes were quite similar to the nations, whereas college-educated families had quite dissimilar preferences: only two of their favorite programs were also on the nation's Top 10. One could conjecture that if the study had done each year for the eight-year span that *Bewitched* was on for, that *Bewitched* would have been reflective of the nation as a whole, and on both the college-educated families list, as well as the U.S. Top 10 list.

To show that this theory is accurate, another study, done in 1991, indicated *Bewitched* as #38 in the Top 100 Television Series of all time. #37 was *My Three Sons*, and #39 was *Who's The Boss*. The study was controlled by assigning each prime time series points based on the number of seasons the show aired for, as well as the audience size ranking each year.

It was not surprising that the series was ranked #38 in the Top 100 Television Series of all time. *Bewitched* averaged a 21.6 audience share throughout its eight seasons, and in January of 1968 gained a daytime rerun audience of 17 million people. This made 52 million people (total daytime and nighttime audience) tuning into Samantha's Sorcery Show. A 1969 *Good Housekeeping* article labeled the show, "one of the most agreeable shows on the air." The article also predicted that *Bewitched* would be among the top shows in its sixth season on the air.

Bewitched is one of the world's most beloved supernatural situation comedies. Its popularity spans cultures and generations. It can be seen in reruns in countries such as England, France, Australia, and Japan. In 2004, Bewitched was released on DVD in Japan and became available in the United States in 2005. Four seasons of Bewitched have been released onto DVD, with a special box set of all eight years being released sometime in the Fall of 2007. In France, they call *Bewitched*, *La Sorceress de bien aimee*, translated it means the well loved witch. It goes to show that misadventure, love, and laughs are synonymous in any language.

With the enormous popularity of the series, it is surprising that *Bewitched* only received three Emmys, even though they were nominated 22 times. William Asher was presented with an Emmy on May 22, 1966, in the category of outstanding Directorial Achievement in a Comedy. Also in 1966, Alice Pearce received an Emmy for her performance as Gladys Kravitz in the category of Outstanding Performance by an Actress in a Supporting Role in a Comedy. In 1967, Marion Lorne received an Emmy for her portrayal as Aunt Clara, in the supporting actress in a Role in Comedy division; it was the last Emmy that a cast member from *Bewitched* received.

Bewitched's premise was rather simple. It was about a witch who marries a mortal, hence a mixed marriage is created. (The first one in Samantha's family). The show wasn't all so strange and unusual. After all, Wilbur had a talking horse, *(Mr. Ed)* The Addams had a walking hand, *(The Addams Family)* and Topper had a houseful of ghosts.

The format of *Bewitched* was rather simple also. It was a variation of the same theme: Samantha (and/or Sam's relatives such as Endora, Arthur, Serena, etc.) gets Darrin (or some other mortal) into trouble brought on by witchcraft. They have a half an hour to try and return sanity and the status quo back to the Stephen's household. *Bewitched* plots usually centered around six mishaps or occurrences.

The first occurrence was Gladys Kravitz (world's nosiest neighbor) witnessing something she isn't supposed to see, such as a manifestation of a spell and then trying to convince her husband that Samantha Stephens (and/or her Sam's relatives) is a witch. "Abbbner!" was Glady's primal scream to her husband anytime she witnessed anything unusual at the Stephens's household.

In Episode #137, "*Samantha's Secret Saucer,*" Aunt Clara zaps up a real flying saucer with Dog men from the planet Parenthia into Samantha's backyard. Gladys sees this happen, and runs home to tell Abner.

Gladys: "An invasion! Right in our neighborhood."
Abner: "Your mother's back?"
Gladys: "In the Stephens's backyard."
Abner: "I'd rather have her over there than here."
Gladys: "It's not my mother!" "It's a flying saucer."
Abner: "You know what I think?" I think your curlers
    are wound too tight."

The second mishap that *Bewitched* often centered around is Uncle Arthur's practical jokes and the chaos that occurs as a result. An example of this can be found in Episode #218, "*The House That Uncle Arthur Built.*" Arthur transfers all of his practical jokes to the Stephens's house to try and impress a snobbish witch by the name of Aretha who detests practical jokes. Sam's house turns into an amusement park fun house. Luckily, the client believes the chaos is for his benefit and Arthur realizes that Aretha isn't worth changing over.

The third occurrence is Aunt Clara's mixed up spells, which she can never figure out how to undo. Poor Aunt Clara, she always had the best intentions for Samantha (Samantha is her favorite niece after all) and Darrin, but somehow her dwindling powers created the worst mistakes, that usually resulted in disasters. Examples of Aunt Clara's disasters can be seen in Episode #87, when she calls on Ben Franklin to help fix a light bulb and can't send him back; and in Episode #100, Clara wants to return to the Victorian era and instead winds up beckoning the overpowering, bossy Queen Victoria to the present day.

As stated earlier, Aunt Clara wants the best for Samantha and Darrin, but she has a hard time deciphering between what is good and bad. In this episode, Larry has almost fired Darrin.

> Samantha: "Darrin may lose his job."
> Aunt Clara: "Oh, I think that's splendid. That way you can
> (to Darrin:) spend more time at home. I just knew it was
> going to be a lucky weekend for both of you."

The fourth mishap is Esmeralda's mixed up spells. Like Aunt Clara, Esmeralda was not a very skilled witch. She was very shy and embarrassed easily; whenever she felt intimidated, she faded or something would pop up accidentally. In Episode #232, "*Samantha's Not-So Leaning Tower of Pisa*," Esmeralda tries to fix a goof, which she had done years earlier. She made the famous Italian city's tower lean, so she restores the historic landmark to its original non-leaning state and cases havoc in Pisa. In Episode #249,"*George Washington Zapped Here*," Esmeralda accidentally zaps up George Washington, to help Tabitha on a school project, and then can't send him back.

The fifth common storyline was Larry firing Darrin whenever a client didn't like a campaign, and Larry taking credit for a slogan when a client did like it. Larry's behavior was always questionable, which can be seen in Episode #138, "*The No-Harm Charm*." In #138, Darrin believes himself to be immune to witchcraft. Samantha and Arthur are watching Darrin promote an advertising campaign via witchcraft (Arthur and Sam are invisible) in Larry's office.

> Arthur: "That Larry would throw two ends of a rope to
>   a drowning man."
> Sam: "That's just Larry's way. The hardest thing for
>   for him to give, is in."

The sixth and final predictable premise is Darrin getting zapped into a hapless state, or placed under a spell. Endora is commonly the culprit. In Episode #121, "*My What Big Ears You Have*", Endora overhears a conversation between Darrin and another woman and suspects Darrin of having an affair. She casts a spell on him that makes his ears grow each time he tells a lie. Later in the episode, it is revealed that the lying is to cover up an antique rocking chair that is meant as a surprise for Samantha. In Episode #103, *"It's Wishcraft,"* Endora uses an incantation to put a spell on Darrin for making Samantha cry.

> Endora: "For every tear that you have made my daughter shed, may buckets of water fall on your head."

Changing Social Times

The family situation comedy genre was popular in the fifties with such shows as *The Donna Reed Show, Leave It To Beaver,* and *The Adventures of Ozzie and Harriet,* but the changing times made it necessary for a new slant on television comedies.

The traditional stereotypical families of the 1950's, were replaced in the sixties by shows such as *My Three Sons*, about a widowed father taking care of three boys; *The Beverly Hillbillies* (1962) about an uncultured bunch of poor country folks who discover oil and suddenly become wealthy; and *My Favorite Martian* (1963) about a newspaper reporter who discovers a Martian who becomes his roommate. The world that the fifties comedies portrayed was out of date, it no longer represented the reality that the new generation would be confronted with.

The 1960's brought with it much tragedy and turbulence with little triumph. At 1:30 p.m. Eastern standard time, on Friday, November 22, 1963, the unthinkable happened, President Kennedy had been shot. This was also the day *Bewitched* began production of the pilot episode. Two days after the announcement of President Kennedy's assassination, Lee Harvey Oswald, the accused assassin, was shot and killed before a nationwide television audience. In these dark days, it became clear that television had the capability to inform, unify, and it became an integral part of daily living.

Before the commencement of *Bewitched* in the fall 1964 lineup, television once again played an imminent role in Americans' lives-this time in the 1964 Presidential Campaign. The Democratic Party used negative imagery in commercials to bombast Goldwater, the Republican candidate for President. As a result, the Democratic Party won by a landslide.

With the swearing in of the new President, Americans were hoping for a brighter future, and a return to normalcy. *Bewitched*, the escapist's adventure, was just what the doctor ordered. On its debut in 1964, *Bewitched* went to #2 in the Nielson Ratings, beating out such popular sitcoms as: *The Andy Griffith Show*, *The Dick Van Dyke Show*, *The Lucy Show*, and *The Beverly Hillbillies*. *Bewitched* quickly gained 31 percent of the audience share, which meant that 31 percent of the television population tuned into the show each week. That same year, Time magazine labeled the comedy, "the runaway champion of all the new TV shows."

This sense of normalcy and optimism was short lived in Americans lives as the 1965 season began. The Vietnam War started to escalate. Another conflict was also occurring simultaneously, the Los Angeles Watts riots had erupted. Once again, television cameras were there to report on the violence and hate. Americans were feeling tense. No longer were they safe; there was violence on their back doorsteps. Because Americans felt their sons and daughters were in jeopardy, the television sitcom became an integral part of daily family life. It was a medication: part humor, fantasy, and escapism. It was just what the doctor ordered.

Through the eight years the show was on, many tragic loses occurred. The Reverend Dr. Martin Luther King Jr., a foremost authority on civil rights, and against violence as a means to unify races, was assassinated. An assassin also gunned down Senator Robert Kennedy. With all of the chaos and despair in an era with a magnitude of loses, *Bewitched* was the magic that was missing in so many American's realities.

Amidst all of the unrest, there were some important historical events that took place. In 1969, the first lunar landing was televised, with Neil Armstrong commander of the Apollo 11 Shuttle walking on the moon. Agnes Moorehead was invited by NASA to witness this moon shot, because as Endora she'd visited the moon many times.

As the turbulent sixties came to a close, television demonstrated its ability to tackle tough social and political issues. Diahann Caroll starred in *Julia*, the first situation comedy in which a black single woman played a leading role. Julia was a story about Julia Baker, a widowed nurse who worked in an aerospace company in the medical department, while also raising her young son, Corey.

The hippie era was just beginning at the end of the sixties. A new political agenda was created. Young people choosing lifestyles different than the ones their parents had expected. Long hair, rock and roll, free love, peace, and communal living were just some of the features of the hippie lifestyle.

Bewitched reflected the changing developments of the time. The transition of the free-spirit mod twin cousin of Samantha, Serena, is an example. When Serena was first introduced as a character on the show, she was more seductive, and she slowly changed into a hippie. In January of 1968, *TV Guide* featured Elizabeth Montgomery dressed in groovy garb on the cover, with the caption reading, "Elizabeth Montgomery Turns Hippie in *Bewitched*."

By the end of the sixties women were changing. The women's movement was off the ground. Women started questioning their roles as wives, daughters, and mothers.

Samantha was a model of the modern, but not yet liberated sixties woman. She was an outlet for women who were faced for the first time with the dilemma of going to work or staying home and raising the kids. Samantha made the role of housewife look exciting; she broke through the boundaries of being a housebound wife, through the mastery of magic.

Bewitched was alluring to the audience in the sixties and early seventies because it provided what the world they lived in was lacking, stability. Every Thursday for seven years, (until 1971, when the day of broadcast was changed to Wednesdays) one could tune into *Bewitched* and forget about the rigors of reality for half an hour.

Copycat Shows

As a result of *Bewitched*'s popularity, CBS and NBC networks tried to replicate the magic. CBS in September of 1965, came out with *Happily Ever After*, shot at the Metro Goldwyn-Mayer studio. It was a musical comedy starring Shirley Jones as a mind reading housewife.

NBC countered by introducing a pretty blonde genie named, Jeannie, on September 18th 1965.

The show was about an astronaut named Tony Nelson (played by Larry Hagman), who came across an old bottle when he crash-landed in the South Pacific. When he opened the bottle, out popped a 2,000-year-old genie, played by Barbara Eden. Jeannie immediately accepted Tony as her master.

Tony decided to take Jeannie back to Florida on three conditions: that she keep her identity a secret, that she refrain from using her magical powers, and that she grant Tony no wishes. However, Tony's co-worker, Roger Healey (Bill Daily) found out about Jeannie's special powers, and was intrigued at the thought of obtaining anything he desired (via wishes).

Besides Tony dealing with Jeannie and Roger, he also was the object of fascination by Dr. Alfred Bellows (Hayden Rorer), the psychiatrist at the NASA base where Tony worked.

Jeannie's efforts to serve her master resulted in confusing situations, she kept Tony's life in a constant state of turmoil with her attempts to better his lot in life.

I Dream of Jeannie was NBC's clone of ABC's *Bewitched*. The premise was the same: Jeannie gets Tony (or some other human) into trouble, leaving her or Tony to get them out of whatever mess she caused with her magic.

Like the witches and warlocks on *Bewitched*, Jeannie was last nameless. (with the exception of Dr. Bombay on *Bewitched*, he didn't have a first name)

Jeannie had an evil twin sister, named Jeannie, which was Barbara Eden in a long black wig. Evil Jeannie was always tried to stir up trouble and flirt with Tony. Evil Jeannie caused problems as did Samantha's mod look-alike cousin, Serena. Serena had short black hair and was played by Elizabeth Montgomery. Jeannie employed magic by blinking her eyes and crossing her arms, whereas, Samantha, twitched her nose.

The similarities to *Bewitched* were uncanny. *On I Dream of Jeannie*, Tony worked with a suspicious psychiatrist by the name of Dr. Alfred Bellows, who pondered, observed, and recorded Tony's every move. On *Bewitched*, the Stephen's had a very suspicious and noisy neighbor, Gladys Kravitz, who was always trying to convince her husband that Samantha Stephens was a witch. Of special note, On *I Dream of Jeannie*, Jeannie had a bottle to go to, and Samantha had Cloud 9 retreat to. *I Dream of Jeannie* even devised the same animated opening credit sequence as *Bewitched*.

Animated Versions

Not only were networks eager to install "witchly" comedies in their prime time programming, they were also interested in introducing charming cartoon versions to the Saturday morning crowd of younger viewers.

An animated version of *I Dream of Jeannie*, called *Jeann*ie, aired Saturday mornings on CBS from September 1973 to August 1975. CBS also came out with another magical character by the name of Sabrina. *Sabrina, the Teen-Age Witch* debuted on September 11, 1971 and ended September 1, 1973. Sabrina first appeared in Archie's Madhouse Comics in 1962. Sabrina, an apprentice witch, was a student of Riverdale High and a classmate of Archie and the gang. She also starred in another Saturday morning series called, *Sabrina and the Groovy Goolies* from 1970-1971, which featured Sabrina with ghouls such as Frankenstein and Dracula.

Like Samantha, Sabrina was anxious to use her powers to assist those in need, but wanted her special powers keep quiet, for fear of ridicule and rejection.

In 1973, (after Bewitched ended) Hanna Barbara introduced a Saturday morning cartoon entitled, *"Tabitha and Adam and the Clown Family."* It aired one time and was about the Stephens children singing in a circus.

Hanna Barbara had more luck with their charming interpretations of resident witch Samantha and hubby Darrin in the mid-sixties with their appearance in the popular Stone Age cartoon, *The Flintstones*. The episode was entitled, *"The Flintstones Meet Samantha."*

The episode started out with the Stephens family moving in across the street from the Flintstones. Darrin has gone on a boating excursion with a client and tells Samantha that the trip would be too strenuous for her. Sam is left alone to unpack their belongings. Wilma and Betty decide to welcome their new neighbor. When they visit Samantha, they tell her that their husbands, Fred and Barney, also are out of town. They wanted to go camping with their husbands but were told ladies weren't invited because it would be too rigorous on women. Samantha used the power of persuasion to convince Wilma and

Betty that women can do anything men can do, and better. The remainder of the episode had Samantha being mischievous by employing witchcraft, (remember it's for a cause) but in the end, she does convince the men that women can do anything men can do.

Brief Series History

Tammy Grimes, the English stage and film actress was initially approached about playing Samantha on *Bewitched*. At the time, she had just signed a deal with Screen Gems TV. She didn't care for the plot or the script for *Bewitched*, so she turned it down in favor of another concept. The other concept became known as *The Tammy Grimes Show*. Unfortunately, *The Tammy Grimes Show* was among the shortest-lived sitcoms in history. It lasted exactly one month.

By luck, or coincidence, Elizabeth Montgomery and William Asher (director of *Our Miss Brooks, The Danny Thomas Show, I Love Lucy, and The Dinah Shore Show*) had recently married and were looking for a project that they could work on together. The project they chose was *Bewitched*, and the rest is history.

There was just one little problem in the beginning, Elizabeth was pregnant at the time the show was sold to Chevrolet and Quaker Oaks, whose advertising agency executives nervously began counting the days until childbirth. The Asher's baby was scheduled to arrive on July 21st, already well beyond the date that most television series had gone into production.

Mr. Asher decided to film every scene in the pilot and the first five episodes around Elizabeth's' pregnant condition. Once the baby arrived, Elizabeth knew that if she didn't report to work as soon as possible, there could be problems. Against doctor's orders, she reported on the set as Samantha exactly 24 days after giving birth.

Success though does have its price. The maddening schedule, upwards of 70 hours a week would be enough to emotionally and physically exhaust most individuals. Elizabeth though was brought up in a show business family, and learned early what the term "trouper" meant. Elizabeth accomplished a miracle, she was not absent from the *Bewitched*'s cast of characters, not even for one segment, nor did she slow down production.

Of course, there is a sweeter side to success. The Asher's owned a substantial percentage of the show's profits and also shared in the merchandising rights for *Bewitched* products.

CHAPTER 2

Seeing Double, The Two Darrin's

"I could zap up mink coats all day long, but I could never zap up another Darrin Stephens".-Samantha talking to Darrin from Episode #99, "Charlie Harper, Winner"

One of the biggest changes on *Bewitched* to go unannounced occurred at the end of the 1968-1969 season. In 1969, without the general audiences' knowledge, Dick York left *Bewitched* and was replaced by Dick Sargent to play the role of Darrin Stephens. The changing of the Darrin's confused many loyal fans because there was no public explanation for the switch. The confusion resulted in *Bewitched* dropping thirteen notches in the ratings when Sargent came on board in the show's sixth season.

At the time of the switch Dick Sargent said, "I don't know why York quit the show, I just thank God that he did."

Dick Sargent had been considered for the role of Darrin when the show was originally cast in 1963, but was under contract to Universal at the time. Sargent was second choice after York for the role, so when it became necessary to find a replacement for York, Dick Sargent was selected. Actor Richard Crenna was also under consideration when the show was originally cast.

It was baffling that a main character would leave a show and no one was offering any reason for the departure. Elizabeth Montgomery and William Asher said, "We were sorry when Dick York bowed out, but Sargent is a wonderful fellow with great talent, and a joy to work with. The loyalty, the family feeling on the set is great." (*Good Housekeeping*, 1969)

The first show that aired with Sargent as Darrin was Episode #171, "Samantha and the Beanstalk". Tabitha over hears her parents discussing names for the new baby and decides that Samantha and Darrin like boys better than girls. Tabitha is jealous of the upcoming arrival, so she decides to run away and switch places with the storybook character Jack, (Johnny Whitaker) from the *Jack and the Beanstalk* storybook. Darrin panics as his mother talks with Jack, and Samantha follows her daughter into the story. In the end, Sam, Tabitha, and Jack return to their proper places.

Dick Sargent's Darrin is first seen swinging a golf club in Episode #171. His first line is: "Sam, how many times have I told you, never talk in the middle of somebody's back swing." However, the first episode that Dick Sargent actually filmed was Episode #185, "Samantha's Better Halves."

Dick Sargent was not the only new arrival in the show's sixth season. Sargent became a father after five episodes with the birth of Adam. (Born on telecast, October 16, 1969). The gender of Adam was kept a secret until the TV birth. According to Bill Asher, "Viewers will find out when Samantha and Darrin do, like in real life." (*Good Housekeeping* October, 1969) This was a precedent started on the *I Love Lucy* Show that Bill Asher was a part of. When Lucille Ball became pregnant, the producers and actors decided to write the pregnancy and new baby into the script. Just as Lucy gained a television offspring a few months after her real life son was born, Elizabeth Montgomery and William Asher's last two children were added to *Bewitched*'s cast of characters. The Asher's first child, Willie, had no television counterpart. He was born two weeks before *Bewitched* started filming in 1964.

Dick York left because of a serious back ailment and a degenerating spine disorder. He injured his back while filming the 1959 western, *They Came to Condura*. In December of 1958, York and others were required to work on a scene for the movie. One of the stunts required that some men lift a car. When the director said cut, all of the men but York had let go of the car. This resulted in severe back pain.

Bewitched filmed twelve to fourteen hours a day, the shooting often dragged behind schedule. There was a lot of pressure that came along with fourteen-hour days. The cast was in agreement when Elizabeth Montgomery said, "When you come to the end of a shooting day, you're beat." (Look, 1965). Due to the pressure of long work hours and pain from a chronic back injury, York developed a drug addiction to pain medication. Unreliable and unpredictable on the set, hastened his already imminent departure. He missed a total of fourteen episodes in two years because of his sickness. (For a complete listing of the shows York was absent from, please refer to the section entitled, **Shows Dick York Missed.**)

Because the premise of the show was about a man married to a witch and all of the chaos surrounding that situation, it put a strain on the show's writers and creators when Darrin was absent. When York was away, what the show decided to do was compensate by inviting other characters to come into the Stephens' household such as: Aunt Clara, Endora, and Serena. This decreased the need to have Darrin constantly in the picture. Many have argued that the episodes that York was absent from just didn't work as well as the ones he was in. His sense of timing, comic relief and ability to utilize extreme facial expressions, made the show so appealing. He also had such a brilliant way to show his affection for Samantha, that when he was absent, "the love story" had to be placed on hold.

York eventually did quit pain pills cold turkey in 1971, but his spine still continued to degenerate and cause him problems. York's back problems prevented him from acting. He managed however to make a few brief guest appearance like in 1983 TV shows *Simon & Simon*.

The summer before Sargent took over the role of Darrin Stephens, he went on tour to promote *Bewitched*. He explained in *TV Guide* that the reason he went on tour was so the country could get a look at the new Darrin. According to Sargent, "While on tour I read a headline one day. The headline read: "Dick York Becomes Darrin." (*TV Guide*, 1970).

It would be difficult to ignore the uncanny resemblance that Dick York and Dick Sargent share. People have very distinct opinions on the way York played Darrin verses Sargent. While both were seasoned actors with various credits to their names, they played Darrin very differently. Dick York seemed to play a very physical Darrin, constantly using eye movements and gestures to get his agitated state across. Sargent was slightly more detached and abrupt and less agile in his movements.

Impact on Today

Today, the changing of the Darrin's has continued to be a topic of conversation and of stand up comedian's jokes. Many nightclub comedians have used the dual Darrin joke in their acts. The 1991 super hit movie, *Wayne's World* made comments about the two Darrin's. Also, game shows such as Jeopardy, Trivial Pursuit and Truth or Dare have asked questions about the Darrin switch.

Chapter 3

Character Traits

Samantha Stephens

"I belong to the greatest minority of them all, I'm a witch"-Samantha, from Episode #164, "The Battle of the Burning Oak".

Character Profile:
Profession: Housewife
Marital Status: Married to Darrin since 1964
Address: 1164 Morning Glory Circle
City: Westport, Connecticut
Age: Not known for sure, but was born somewhere around 1600.
Children: Tabitha, born on January 13, 1966, and Adam, born on October 16, 1969
Parents: Endora and Maurice
Favorite Resort Spot: Cloud #9
Nickname: Sam and Sammy

By occult standards, Samantha Stephens is a dropout witch who yearns to be a housewife and desires to please her mortal husband Darrin, by abstaining from witchcraft. It isn't powers Samantha desires; it's domesticity, with Darrin as head of the household. Samantha is content with her choice to curb her magical appetite, in favor of a more palatable seasoning, love.

There are two main features of Samantha's character that are seen in great detail. The first is Samantha's compassion for others, and the second is her strength coupled with her intelligence.

Samantha Stephens is a compassionate person who uses her "twitch" for worthy causes.

In Episode #6, "Little Pitchers Have Big Fears", Samantha boosts a young boys' confidence (named Marshall Burns) and convinces his overprotective mother to allow him to play baseball.

The trend follows in Episode #23, "Red Light, Green Light". Samantha and Darrin plan a rally to convince the mayor that a traffic signal is needed at the busy Morning Glory Circle intersection. After getting magically delayed in traffic, the mayor decides to approve a traffic signal.

Finally, in Episode #90, Soap Box Derby", Samantha once again shows her compassion. Samantha comes to the aid of a boy with an unsupportive father. She helps young Johnny Miller prepare for a Soap Box Derby. When Johnny wins the race, he is accused of cheating. Samantha helps a once reluctant father to come to the defense of his son and Johnny is cleared of all charges.

Episodes #149 "Samantha Fights City Hall" as well as #213 "Sisters at Heart", demonstrate Samantha's strength and intelligence in handling challenging situations.

In Episode #149, "Samantha Fights City Hall", Samantha is determined to save a neighborhood playground from being demolished and turned into a shopping center. She and other mothers decide to stage a protest. Darrin suggests to Sam that she give up the project due to unforeseen circumstances (his client is the developer). Instead, Samantha sticks to her principles and sees the project through to completion. In one scene, Darrin says to Sam: "It's just Willow Street Park, not Dunkirk." Samantha's' retort is one of steadfast desire to keep with the project. At the end of the episode, Darrin realizes how special Samantha is and says: "You're a witch in a million!"

Another episode in which Samantha is shown as a compassionate individual is Episode #213, "Sisters at Heart". Tabitha and her black friend Lisa are hurt by a prejudice remark that they overheard as a result, they decide they want to become sisters. Tabitha's wishcraft spell accidentally produces black polka dots on Tabitha and white ones on Lisa. As Samantha goes in search of Dr. Bombay, she leaves Lisa's mother in charge. Darrin's client, Mr. Brockway mistakes Lisa's mom for Darrin's wife and quickly changes his tune concerning giving Darrin the account. Samantha shows the bigoted Mr. Brockway as well as the girls' that you don't have to look alike to be sisters. More importantly, it is what is in your heart.

In Episode #99, "Charlie Harper Winner", Darrin's college buddy Charlie Harper is rich and successful. His wife Daphne is snobby, materialistic, and envious. Despite having worldly goods—a castle, jewelry, a maid, a butler, expensive clothes and perfumes, nothing seems to satisfy Daphne. Samantha zaps up a mink coat to impress Daphne, but the plan backfires and the greedy Daphne demands that her husband purchase the mink for her. Samantha, fearing that Darrin will believe himself inferior to Charlie Harper, decides to give the mink to Daphne. Daphne: "You can't give away anything valuable." Samantha (directing her comments to Darrin) "Oh, yes you can. When you value something else a great deal more! Daphne: "More than this, oh you're kidding. Samantha: No, I'm not. I don't think I've ever been as serious or meant anything as much in my life!" Darrin: "Oh, Sam."(Sam and Darrin kiss)

I believe that this brief interchange was at the crux of Samantha's value system. Samantha's motto can be interpreted as people are unequivocally more valuable than possessions, in fact, people are priceless.

Sam's Most Characteristic Lines:
"Witchcraft got you into this mess, witchcraft will get you out."
"Weeell"
"Oh, my stars!"
"Okay, who's the wise witch?"
"I think you've cracked your cauldron."

Samantha Trivia

Samantha says "weeelll" twice each in episodes #44, #52, #53, #86, #92, #130, #192, #203, #214.
Samantha promises to "never use witchcraft again" in Episode #53, "Maid to Order".
Samantha gives Darrin a watch for his birthday as seen in Episode #167, "Daddy Does His Thing".
In a heated moment of temporary anger, Samantha tells Darrin that she knew Plato and Socrates, but then she later denies it. She recounts by saying, "I wasn't even born yet!" (#252, "A Good Turn Never Goes Unpunished.")
Samantha wore a pink wool dress on their first date. (#198, "Mona Sammy".)
Samantha is fluent in Italian (as evidenced in Episodes #110, 155, 156, 232), Spanish (Episode #170), German (Episode #231), and French (#234), but not in Japanese (Episode #136)
In "Humbug Not To Be Spoken Here", and in "Samantha's Curious Cravings", Samantha calls Larry Tate a son of a gun.
In the season two opener, #37, "Alias Darrin Stephens", Samantha tells Darrin that she is pregnant with Tabitha.

In Episode #232, "Samantha's Not So Leaning Tower of Pisa", Samantha uses some Italian in reference to Esmeralda's unusual behavior by saying, "Buffa, Buffa". Buffa, Buffa is the feminine form of the Italian word "buffo", which translated into English means funny or comical.

We discover that Samantha learned to play the lute as a child from Episode #229, "How Not To Lose Your Head to Henry the VII"(part one).

Samantha Stephens Trivia

1. Samantha's mom and dad are:
    a. Phyllis and Frank
    b. George and Martha
    c. Endora and Maurice

2. Samantha's favorite resort spot is:
    a. Cloud 9
    b. Cloud 13
    c. The Moon

3. Samantha Stephens profession is:
    a. Housekeeper
    b. Maid
    c. Housewife

4. Samantha's children's names are:
    a. David and Darrin
    b. Tabitha and Adam
    c. Endora and Maurice

5. Samantha's birthday is:
    A. April the 15th
    B. June the 6th
    C. October 31st

6. In Episode #70, "Man's Best Friend", Samantha says she hasn't done witchcraft in:
   A. one week
   B. 29 days
   C. one month

7. In Episode #65, "Disappearing Samantha", Samantha and Endora give Osgood Rightmire
   A. The Male Warlock of the Year Award
   B. A bad time
   C. The Ordeal By Fire Warlock Test

8. In Episode #71, "The Catnapper", Samantha flies around the world looking for:
   A. Endora
   B. Uncle Arthur
   C. Maurice

9. Samantha is the first witch in over ___ years to take the tower tour of King Henry the VIII's castle? (answer can be found in Episode #229, "How Not to Lose Your Head to Henry VIII", part I)
   A. 200 years
   B. 400 years
   C. 100 years

10. In Episode #219, "Samantha and the Troll", Samantha goes to the doctor for her
    A. 10,000 spell checkup and overhaul
    B. A pregnancy Test
    C. Voracious Ravenousitis

Samantha Stephens answers:
1. C. Endora and Maurice; 2. A. Cloud 9; 3. C. Housewife; 4. B. Tabitha and Adam; 5. B. June 6th

Darrin Stephens

Character Profile:
Profession: Advertising Executive
Place of work: McMann & Tate
Marital Status: Married to Samantha since 1964
Pet Peeve: The use of witchcraft and seeing his mother-in-law Endora
Dislikes: Samantha's family
Home Phone: 555-7328, 555-2134, or 555-2368
Favorite Dish: Beef Stew
Parents: Phyllis and Frank
Hobbies: Golf and drinking at Joe's Bar and Grill

Darrin is a typical 1960s white-collar worker who tries to get ahead by showing creativity and a good work ethic. Darrin is undervalued and unappreciated by his domineering boss Larry Tate. Even in his own domicile, he gets little respect from Samantha's family. His mother-in-law Endora's constant presence and interference compounds the problems.

In Episode #82, "Dangerous Diaper Dan", Darrin and Samantha have an argument and this is what transpires.
Samantha: "I have a good mind to go home to mother."
Darrin: "What for? Your mother is always here!"

Darrin was set up for failure from the start. He could never measure up to Samantha's relatives expectations, simply because he was mortal.

Darrin feared that Sam's family was right, that he wasn't a sufficient provider. As a result, he often felt insecure and inadequate, so every time Samantha used her powers, this diminished his self-esteem even further.

Darrin's coping mechanisms to deal with his perceived shortcomings included blowing off steam by yelling, partaking in adult beverages, and hitting the greens. The usage of defense mechanisms showed that Darrin was only human, not perfect, and that Samantha married him because she loved him—warts and all.

Cocktails at 5:00
As stated above, one of Darrin's coping mechanisms to deal with the mayhem, would be to retreat to Joe's Bar and Grill. He often would tell his woes to a lonely drunkard.

Darrin: "My wife's a witch, my mother-in-law is a witch, I'm surrounded by them."
Drunk: "You ought to see my mother-in-law, she has fangs."
(Samantha pops into the bar)
Samantha: "Darrin, are you coming home?"
Darrin: "No."
Drunk: "Well, she doesn't look like a witch to me!"
Darrin: "Well, she is!!!"

Eventually, in his inebriated state, he would find his way home.

Darrin: "Good evening Samantha. Good evening madam."
Sam: "Darrin?"
Darrin: "Don't you recognize me either?"
Sam: "What's wrong?"
Endora: "He's sauced to the gill."
Sam: "Mother please!"
Darrin: "Nonsense madam, I'm quite sober. I only had tee martinis."
Sam: "Well you better take the olives out of your mouth, cause you're talking funny."
Endora: "Funny is better than dreary."
Darrin: "Would you kindly tell little Miss Muffet to get her tuffet out of here!"
Endora: "Alright, but if you need me just light a match near his breath, I'll see the flames."
Darrin: "Good old Smokey the bore."

Darrin's Most Characteristic Lines:
"I wish you wouldn't call him that!" (In reference to Samantha calling Dr. Bombay, "the witch doctor".)
"Samm!!!"

In Episode #1, "I, Darrin, Take This Witch Samantha", Darrin is said to be Vice-President of McMann and Tate, rather than Account Executive. In Episode 1, his personal secretary is named Helen, instead of Betty (as seen in later episodes).
When Darrin was twenty-three years old, he won a paper airplane contest (Episode #154, "Samantha's Super Maid".)
We find out in Episode #233, "Bewitched, Bothered and Baldoni", that Darrin's favorite eye color is green.

Unfortunately, Darrin gets arrested in Episodes #42, 204,and 253.

When Endora turns Darrin into a snob in Episode #164, "The Battle of Burning Oak", we discover that Darrin's taste buds change. His snobbish side prefers chateaubriand and Lobster Newburg.

The only one to ever appreciate and like Louise Tate's coffee is Darrin. (from Episode #59, "Double Tate").

Darrin's secretary Betty's last name is Wilson (Episode #153, #157) and she was born in St. Paul, from "The Girl With The Golden Nose".

In Episode #139, "Man of Year", the Hucksters Club names Darrin, "Advertising Man of the Year". Mr. McMann won the title back in 1943 by starting the first Advertising Man of the Year, and by electing himself.

Darrin dreams that his has five witch/warlock children in Episode #12, "… And Something Makes Three". The children's names are Endora, Maurice, Rebecca, Samuel, and Julius.

We find out in Episode #68, "A Bum Raps", that Darrin doesn't know how to swim.

We discover in Episode #190, "Super Arthur", that Sunday is Darrin's regular golf day.

In Episodes #72, 135, and 211, Darrin spills the beans and tells Larry that Samantha is a witch.

Through the eight seasons on Bewitched, Darrin has been turned into a newspaper ("Just One Happy Family"), a penguin (appeared in episode "George the Warlock"), a chimp (Episode #37), a gorilla (as seen in Episode #222, "Darrin Goes Ape"), a mule (Episode #167, "Daddy Does His Thing"), a goose ("Long Live the Queen", and "Samantha and the Antique Doll"), a statue (Episode #145, "It's So Nice to have a Spouse Around the House", Episode #205, "Darrin on a Pedestal", and Episode #234, "Paris, Witch's Style"), a frog (Episode #201, "To Go, or not to Go that is the Question), a dog (Episode #199), a crow (Episode #208, "Samantha's Old Salem Trip"), a goat (Episode #158), a kidd/baby goat (Episode #225, "Samantha's Psychic Slip"), a pig's head (Episode #220, "This Little Piggy"), and a boy (Episode #46, and #224), just to name some.

Darrin's cousin Helen comes for a visit with her fiancée to Darrin and Samantha's house as seen in Episode #129, "A Prince For a Day", but quickly falls for Prince Charming.

Darrin Stephens

1. Darrin's place of employment
   A. McMann & Tate
   B. McMann, Tate, & Stephens
   C. Meyers and Son

2. Darrin married Samantha in what year?
   A. 1957
   B. 1963
   C. 1964

3. Darrin's main pet peeve is
   A. The use of witchcraft
   B. Senile people
   C. Clowns

4. Darrin's' mom and dad are
   A. Homer and Marge
   B. Mike and Carol
   C. Phyllis and Frank

5. Darrin's favorite meal consists of:
   A. Beef Stew
   B. Black Bean Soup
   C. Chicken Pot Pie

Answers: 1. A. McMann & Tate; 2. C. 1964; 3. A. The Use of Witchcraft; 4. C. Phyllis and Frank; 5. A. Beef Stew

Endora

<u>Character Profile</u>
Friends: Hagatha and Enchantra
Marital Status: Married to Maurice, but it is an informal hook up.
Favorite Dish: Coq au vin
Hobbies: Loves traveling all around the world, and to the moon too!
Dislikes: Darrin, and most mortals
Likes: Making Darrin's (and/or other mortals) lives miserable.
Pet Peeve: She is upset that her daughter Samantha settled for a mere mortal and wants Samantha to find a warlock and live a free-spirited witchly life.

Endora is a sophisticated free spirit who uses her powers to taste all of the cultural and sensual delights that the universe has to offer. Endora clearly enjoys being a witch and can't comprehend why Samantha would prefer to hide her powers, perform tedious household tasks, and endure Darrin's constant tirades.

Endora is a confident strong willed witch. She embraces her witchly heritage; however, she is unaware that she embodies human qualities. too. Her more human, stereotypical mother-in-law side can be seen in Episode #118. In this episode, Endora looses her powers, and her vulnerability is exposed.

(From Episode #118, "Allergic to Macedonian Dodo Birds")

Endora in a weak state with a frail voice: "Is Tabitha still in her room?"
Samantha: "Aahaa."
Endora: "What's the big attraction there?"
Darrin: "Privacy."
Endora: "You meant that as an insult, didn't you?"
Samantha: "No mother, he didn't mean it."
Endora: "He hates me!"
Samantha: "Mother, he doesn't hate you, do you Darrin?"
Endora. "He does too. I'll have to live out my life in a climate of hatred."
Darrin: "What do you mean live out your life?"
Endora: "Have you forgotten? I'm not leaving this house without me powers."
Darrin: "I never agreed to that. I only agreed to last night. Come sundown I call you a cab—right?"

Samantha: "Weelll"
Darrin: "Well, what?"
Samantha: "Who will take care of her?"
Darrin: "We can put her in a home for senior citizens. And when you're a senior citizen as much as she must be, they'll give her the best room in the house."
Samantha: "Darrin, we can't do that. She's my mother."
Darrin: "And I'm your husband."
Endora: "She could divorce you."
Darrin: "She could turn you into a parakeet and we could keep you in a cage."

A few minutes later, Darrin says, "If she doesn't leave, I will." Samantha asks, "For how long?" Darrin decides to use one of his coping mechanisms, retreating to the local bar. Samantha tries to convey to Darrin that Endora considers herself helpless without her powers. Later in the episode, the reason is discovered for her loss of powers. She discovers that her powers have been transferred to Aunt Clara due to an allergy to Macedonian dodo birds. Tabitha had zapped one up out of one of her books. Once Dr. Bombay comes up with an antidote, Endora's powers are regained, as is her wicked disposition.

Endora's Most Characteristic Lines
"What Mother knows best is how to prove she's right!"
"Oh, Samantha ... really!"
"I'll say it once and only once, I was wrong and I'm sorry."-Endora apologizing to Samantha and Darrin
"Look how well she sleeps up here. It is the lovely smog free air".-Endora talking about Tabitha while she and Samantha are on Cloud 8.

Endora Trivia:
In Episode #43, "Trick or Treat", Endora as a child says that there are over 7000 combinations of magic words.

Endora

1. Endora's favorite dish is:
   A. Chauterbriand
   B. Coq au Vin
   C. Lobster Newburg

2. Endora always has this for breakfast?
   A. Fried Ravens Eggs
   B. Her Witches Special
   C. Poached Eggs

3. Endora's favorite cities are?
   A. Paris and Rome
   B. London and Venice
   C. Rome and Barcelona

4. Endora tells Darrin her last name is:
   A. Very exotic
   B. Smith
   C. Unpronounceable

5. In Episode #132, "To Twitch or Not To Twitch", Endora and Samantha visit
   A. Cloud 9
   B. Cloud 8
   C. Cloud 13

6. In Episode #34, "Remember the Main", Endora says her last name is
   A. Waters
   B. Rivers
   C. Summers

7. In Episode #252, "A Good Turn Never Goes Unpunished", Endora and Samantha have a tall cool one in/on
   A. Cloud 9
   B. Paris
   C. Rome

8. Endora claims to have been at
   A. Stonehenge
   B. Louvre, when they laid the cornerstone
   C. Paris, for the unveiling of the Eiffel Tower

9. Endora mentions that she once told _____ to "Get Lost!"
   A. Bluebeard
   B. Henry VIII
   C. Columbus

10. Endora is this according to Samantha
    A. 5 feet 6 inches tall and 118 pounds
    B. Full of hot air
    C. 5 feet five inches tall and light as a feather

Endora Answers: 1. A. Chauterbriand; 2. A. Fried Ravens Eggs; 3.A. Paris and Rome; 4. C. Unpronounceable; 5. B. Cloud 8; 6. A. Waters; 7. A. Cloud 9; 8. B. Louvre, when they laid the cornerstone; 9. C. Columbus; 10.A. 5 feet 6 inches tall and 118 pounds

Larry Tate

Character Profile
Profession: Partner at McMann & Tate, an Advertising Agency
Passion: Money
Marital Status: Married to Louise
Children: Jon Tate (close to Tabitha's age)
How Larry and Louise got engaged: Larry blew a smoke ring and Louise stuck her finger through it, and said I do. (episode #64)
Larry's Classic Line: "I've always wanted to rule the world, ever since I was a little kid." (episode #135)
Serena's pet name for Larry: Peter Cotton Top.

Manipulative, greedy, credit grabbing, chauvinistic, and irritable all describe the character of Larry Tate. He was a man with a shallow persona who thrived to work. In Episode #135, "I Confess", Larry is told that Samantha is a witch, this is how her reacts:
Larry: "Samantha. with my brains and your voodoo, we can control the world. Today the nation, tomorrow the world."
Darrin: "Larry, take it easy!"
Larry: "I can't, I'm mad with power."

Samantha: "But we're not, we don't want to use my witchcraft to rule the world."
Darrin: "Right, and I'm sure when you've had time to think it over you'll decide"
Larry: "I'll decide I want to rule the world. I've wanted to rule the world ever since I was a little kid."

Many of the Bewitched episodes were centered around the Larry-Darrin-Client triangle.

Often Larry used Darrin as a scapegoat, especially if he anticipated that an account was going south. "You're fired!" is a familiar staple said by Larry to Darrin. The firing of Darrin happened so frequently it made one wonder, "could Larry Tate be so shallow?" Samantha answered this question in Episode #138, "*The No Harm Charm*" while talking to Uncle Arthur.

Arthur: "That Larry would throw two ends of a rope to a drowning man."
Samantha: "That's just Larry's way. The hardest thing for him to give, is in."

Sometimes though Larry would see the error in his ways. In #148, "Is it Magic or Imagination", Larry tries to make amends for falsely firing Darrin.
Larry: "Everybody knows that I'm a volatile, excitable, impetuous, rash, impulsive."
Darrin: "Blowhard?"
Larry: "That wasn't exactly the word I was looking for."
Darrin: "How about hysterical nut?"
Larry "I'll stick with blowhard."

Donald Trump, America's renowned billionaire with his 21st century catch phrase, "You're fired", has made a killing with his new show, *The Apprentice*. Larry Tate could give Donald Trump lessons on when and how to use the phrase, "You're fired!"

Larry Tate lacked self-esteem and imagination. He truly believed he was a rotten husband and father and the only thing that he was reasonably good at was working. As a result, Larry became the classic workaholic, being a boss and McMann's partner gave Larry something to be proud of. His low self-esteem coupled with his fear of failure is probably why Larry never opened up his own advertising agency and was so quick to place blame on Darrin.

He was a brilliant businessman though and he realized that he needed Darrin's creativity.

It may have been business first with Larry, but underneath his shallow façade and rough exterior was a man who deeply cared and valued his family and friendships.

Larry's Most Characteristic Lines

"You son of a Gun."
"You are fired Darrin!"
"Darrin is no longer with McMann &Tate"
"I'm sorry Mr./Miss client _____, as of today Darrin is no longer with McMann & Tate."

Aunt Clara

Character Profile:
Character Trait: Bumbling, shy, and senile
Favorite Pastime: Visiting her niece Samantha, Darrin, and Tabitha.
Pet Peeve: When Endora interferes in Samantha and Darrin's lives.
Marital Status: Clara is an unmarried witch, but has had a few boyfriends throughout the series. Her beau Hedley can be seen in Episode #47, "Aunt Clara's Old Flame", as well as Ocky in Episode #83, "The Short Happy Circuit of Aunt Clara".
Biggest Bother: Clara's inability to get spells done correctly. Also, most of the witches in her social circle ostracize her and keep their distance marriage in order to avoid dealing with their own impending senility.

No one wants to get older, especially witches who are supposed to stay youthful and vibrant forever. Clara is neither youthful nor vibrant which makes her a target of mockery and ridicule among her friends and witchly relatives. The only person who seems to sympathize with Clara's plight is Samantha. Not so odd when one objectively looks at Sam and Clara's vocations in life. Samantha is forbidden to use her witchcraft and Clara is unable to access hers. They both don't practice spells and incantations for different reasons, but their genuine affection for Darrin and each other is evident.

Aunt Clara's Most Characteristic Lines
"Oh, I think that's splendid!"
"Oh no!"

Aunt Clara Trivia

Marion Lorne played a character named Aunt Clara in the 1955 movie: The Girl Rush.

The Magic of Bewitched Trivia

1. Clara says Samantha has Square Green Spots Disease, it lasts one year, but usually witches in what country get it?
   A. Peru
   B. Argentina
   C. Mexico

2. When Aunt Clara meets Darrin for the first time, she fixes what for dinner?
   a. chicken with mushrooms and artichokes with a strawberry sundae
   b. coq au vin and pineapple upside down cake
   c. Veal and lemon meringue pie for dessert.

3. What does Aunt Clara collect?
   a. doorknobs
   b. doorbells
   c. Hangers

4. How many of this item does Clara have in her collection?
   a. 1,000
   b. 3,000
   c. 20,000

5. _____ And Clara were known as the "Golden Couple".
   a. Hedley
   b. Mark
   c. Harry

Answers: 1. A. Peru; 2.B. Coq au Vin with pineapple upside down cake; 3. b. doorknobs; 4. b. 3,000; 5. a. Hedley

Dr. Bombay

Character Profile
Favorite Pastime: Chasing nurses or enjoying one of his many other favorite leisure activities (while being on-call) such as climbing Mt. Everest, scuba diving, climbing the Matterhorn.
Pet Peeve: Anyone who needs his help.

Second Favorite Pastime: Reciting jokes, which he isn't very good at.

What witch family could function without their very own friendly, on-call witch physician, sure to cure whatever doesn't ail you. Unlike most family physicians, doctor Bombay seemed bothered by anyone who actually needed his help.

Dr. Bombay enjoyed the perks associated with being an on-call witch physician. He spent plenty of time occupying himself with buffalo polo, dolphin races, or flirting and chasing one of his many new assistant nurses. There were a slew of new nurses, Samantha couldn't keep track of them all. Whenever one of these nurses would arrive in place of doctor Bombay (who was obviously playing hooky), a I line would be recited:

Nurse: "I'm his new (Dr. Bombay) trained nurse."
Samantha: "Could you help me?"
Nurse: "That's not what I'm trained in."

Dr. Bombay was rarely reachable as he was always too busy with one of his leisurely activities. In order to get a response from the doctor, Samantha often times would have to exclaim, *"Calling Dr. Bombay, emergency, come right away!"* When Samantha and/or Endora would complain about his apparent absences, or goofs, his typical response would be, *"Call me through the exchange."*

Many times when Dr. Bombay would show up, the cure would backfire. Such was the case in Episode #174, *"Samantha's Curious Cravings"*. Samantha called the doctor because whenever she would have a craving for a certain food, it would instantly come to her.

When Bombay supposedly cures her, he merely reverses the situation, instead of the food coming to her, she goes to the food. In the end, Bombay finally helps Samantha with her problem.

<u>Dr. Bombay's Most Characteristic Lines:</u>
"Ha-ha … nothing!"

Uncle Arthur

Character Profile:
Character: Trickster and joker. Enjoys doing pranks, mainly on unsuspecting Darrin. Enjoys spending time with Samantha, Tabitha, and Adam.

Relations: Arthur is Endora's brother. Though he prefers that no one mention this fact. Note: Endora and Arthur have equal powers.
Love Interest: Aretha, a snobbish witch that was seen in Episode #218, "*The House that Uncle Arthur Built*".
Pet Peeve: Being Endora's brother. This is something that he would like to forget, and if possible, change.
Favorite Sport: Riding in the Ostrich Derby. This fact is mentioned in Episode #150, "*Samantha Loses Her Voice.*"
Favorite Sport, Runner Up: Annoying Endora. This is one thing that Darrin and Arthur have in common.
Soft Spot: Like Clara, Uncle Arthur adores his niece Samantha and will do anything to support her, even if it goes against his beliefs. In Episode #165, "*Samantha's Power Failure*", Arthur forfeits his witchcraft when he goes against the Witches' Council demand that Samantha and Darrin's marriage be dissolved.

Paul Lynde made occasional guest appearances on *Bewitched* as Samantha's fun loving and snide warlock uncle named Arthur.

Arthur was a colorful character who loved making jokes at other people's expense. His off color joking can be seen in Episode #150, "Samantha Loses Her Voice". Arthur: (talking about a puppy) "I got him in a thunderstorm. It was raining cats and dogs."

Samantha: "And you stepped in a poodle." Arthur: "Not bad Sammy, but it would have been funnier if I had said it."

Practical joking Uncle Arthur produced many hilarious moments on *Bewitched*, especially in his dealings with his sister Endora. They despised one another, and their apparent dislike may have been due to their distinct personality differences, plus the fact that their witchcraft was equally matched. Endora and Arthur viewed life and situations differently. Endora used her powers in a more reserved fashion, preferring to be a cultural connoisseur, inhaling the exotic delights of the galaxy. Arthur on the other hand, enjoyed corny jokes and making people laugh and or exasperated. Because of the differences between Arthur and Endora, miscommunication was frequent, and often their battles placed Samantha and Darrin in the crossfire.

In Episode #80, "Endora Moves In For A Spell", Arthur and Endora clash over how Tabitha's witchcraft should be guided. During the power struggle, Arthur and Endora zap a house on and off a vacant lot across the street from Sam and Darrin's home. Endora vows never to return. In the interim, Darrin objects to Arthur's' influence on Tabitha and decides that Endora isn't so bad after all. Endora reappears and Samantha forces Arthur and Endora to make up.

    The bickering continues over the house (from Episode #80). Darrin is concerned because Endora wants to throw a lavish Halloween party at the zapped up house. Samantha convinces Endora to remove the dwelling, however, Endora decides to hold her Halloween party at Samantha and Darrin's home, and extravagantly remodels the living room, much to their dismay.
    The party gets off to a grand start, with champagne and exotic delicacies floating about the room. Endora feels confident that the party is a success and decides to recite poetry. Arthur, embarrasses his sister, by making a mockery of her recitation.
Endora: *"Twas the night before Halloween, and all who were chic, were sipping champagne ...*
Arthur: They'd been stoned for a week.
Endora: The witches and warlock in Rome by the score, with their ladies attired in the best by Dior ...
Arthur Were checking their warts as they came through the door.
Endora: And the odd little mortal s all snug in their beds, while visions of trick-or-treat danced in their heads. Our children were practicing spells and their chants ...
Arthur: And even the poltergeists pulled off their pants.
    Endora was so disgusted by Arthur's commentary that she and her party vanish. During this episode, the sibling rivalry is evident. At one point Endora says to Arthur, "You call yourself my brother!" His reply, "Only when I am forced to. I deny it as much as possible."

<u>Uncle Arthur's Most Characteristic Line</u>
"Hiya, Sammy."

Esmeralda

Character Profile
Profession: Witch Maid
Status: Unmarried
Personality: Insecure and lonely
Pet Peeve: Upsetting Darrin and making mistakes

Shy, insecure, and clumsy all describe the character of Esmeralda. Similar to Aunt Clara, Esmeralda had difficulty getting her witchcraft to work correctly. Poor Esmeralda, whenever she sneezed a disaster was lurking around the corner. Luckily, her disasters were only temporary and they usually faded before the close of the episode.

Some of Esmeralda's mishaps have included accidentally conjuring up the Emperor Julius Caesar, zapping up George and Martha Washington, and sneezing up Mother Goose.

The role of Esmeralda was added to the Bewitched cast after Marion Lorne, who portrayed bumbling, senile Aunt Clara passed away. Like Clara, Esmeralda was an example of a less than perfect, but still loveable witch. Much like Glinda the Good Witch from *The Wizard of Oz*, Clara and Esmeralda added balance to the extreme witch characters of Endora, Serena, Hagatha, and Enchantra.

Esmeralda was a retiring wallflower, a well-meaning person in search of love.

In Episode #232, "*Samantha's Not-So-Leaning Tower of Pisa*", it is discovered that Esmeralda had made the tower lean accidentally years earlier while trying to please her boyfriend, Bonano Pisano, the tower's builder. By going back in time, Esmeralda recalls the incident that caused the Tower to lean and decides to redo history. Confident with herself, Esmeralda decides to restore the tower back to its original stature. Much to her dismay, no one else in the tiny town of Pisa is happy that the tower

Esmeralda's quest for love can be seen in Episode #226, "*Samantha's Magic Mirror,*" Esmeralda asks Samantha to assist her with her ailing powers to impress an old warlock boyfriend by the name of Ferdy whom she hasn't dated in over 400 years. To boost Esmeralda's confidence, Samantha bewitches the mirrors in the house so Esmeralda sees herself as a pretty young witch. During the episode, it is discovered that Ferdy also has an assistant and Ferdy's powers prove to be just as deficient as Esmeraldas'. The couple find comfort and humor in their situation.

<u>Esmeralda's Most Characteristic Lines</u>
"Oh, dear!"
"Oh, my!"
"I think I'm going to fade."

Gladys Kravitz

<u>Character Profile</u>
Marital Status: Married to Abner
Maiden Name: Gruber
Children: Gladys has no biological children. She does however have a few nephews who she dotes upon. Gladys' nephews are: Floyd, Edgar, Flash, Tommy, Seymour, and Sidney.
Pet Peeve: No one believing her that Samantha Stephens is a witch.

Suspicious and noisy describe the character of Gladys Kravitz, an amateur detective with an insatiable desire to prove that Samantha Stephens is a witch. Gladys will stop at nothing to prove her point that something just isn't quite right at the Stephens's' household.

A familiar staple of Bewitched is Mrs. Kravitz seeing some manifestation of witchcraft and not getting Abner's attention fast enough for him to see it. This leads Abner to question his wife's' mental state.

Gladys has witnessed Darrin with enormous ears, Darrin shrinking, babies talking, a spaceship with spacemen/dogs, and people flying, just to name a few.

Abner did not validate Gladys's feelings. Most psychologists would agree that even if Gladys were making up stories about Samantha, many of the stories would seem plausible. Abner was in denial over his wife's needs and felt more comfortable in suspecting her as a loony. Their relationship lacked trust and respect. Abner has said to Gladys such things as: *"Have you got that buzzing in your head again?" "That's it, tomorrow she goes to the psychiatrist."*

Though such statements added comic relief on *Bewitched*, who would blame Gladys for wanting to spice up her mundane life with Abner? In Episode #47, "*Aunt Clara's Old Flame*", Abner is seen using selective listening on his wife.
Gladys: "Abner, there is a wizard at the Stephens's' house!"
Abner: "Good for the lawn, it eat mosquitoes."
Gladys: "Not a lizard, a wizard."
Abner: "Wizard, lizard. as long as it eats the mosquitoes."

Gladys Kravitz really was just a bored housewife with a lackluster life who yearned for the excitement that Samantha's life provided. She spent considerably less time with the Stephens family than Larry and Louise Tate, and yet they never caught onto Samantha's secret.

David Keil, a noted Historian on *Bewitched*, summed it up best with his version of what Gladys Kravitz might be doing today. *"Abner and Gladys sold their Morning Glory Circle house and bought a condo in New Jersey. Gladys' book, <u>The Samantha Stephens I Have Known and Feared</u>, was serialized in Cosmopolitan magazine prior to its 1977 publication. It stayed on the New York Times best-seller list for 66 weeks."*

Gladys' Most Characteristic Lines
"Abner, you won't believe what I saw Mrs. Stephens do!"
"Abner, I'm going over to the Stephens to borrow a cup of sugar."
"Mrs. Stephens, what are you doing?"
"Aaabner!!!"

Maurice

Character Profile:
Favorite Pastime: Reciting Shakespeare
Marital Status: Married to Endora, it is an informal marriage.
Residence: Somewhere is England
Grandchildren: Tabitha and Adam
Favorite Drink: Martini with Spanish Gin and Italian Vermouth

Omnipotent, fierce, strong-willed, and elegant describe the character of Maurice, played by Maurice Evans. Samantha's father Maurice is a very proper warlock. He typically wears a top hat and tails when he comes to visit. His manner of speech is rather grand also. He often recites Shakespearian soliloquies, as he is a member of the Shakespearian actors Guild. He resides in England and prefers the finer things in life: beautiful young witches, vintage champagne, and classic cars such as a Rolls-Royce.

Maurice is a very powerful warlock, therefore he is also the most threatening. His power is stronger than Endora's, which makes Darrin likely prey.

In Episode #234, "Paris, Witches Style", Maurice learns of Samantha and Darrin's visit to Paris. He is offended and angered that Darrin and Samantha did not visit him in England. Endora, fearful of what Maurice might do to Darrin, creates a duplicate Darrin, one that is kind, charming, and pleasant to Maurice. It works for a short time, then Maurice catches on to the scheme. In his rage, Maurice zaps the real Darrin to the top of the Eiffel Tower. This is one example of Maurice being unkind to Darrin.

Maurice made no qualms concerning his dislike for Darrin. His reasoning was based upon his impression of all mortals, as an inferior group. Darrin unfortunately was part of that minority and therefore was disliked. In one episode, Maurice even says, "Mortals have as much backbone as earthworms."

<u>Maurice's Most Characteristic Lines</u>
"Something is rotten in the state of Denmark."
"I'm on my way to the Opera."
"How is my beautiful charming daughter?"
"How is Dobbin treating you my dear Samantha."
… Any classic lines from Shakespeare

Maurice Trivia:
Maurice calls Darrin by name in Episode #181, "Darrin the Warlock".

CHAPTER 4

Supernatural Situation Comedy

THE CAST OF BEWITCHED

ROLE	PLAYED BY
Samantha Stephens	Elizabeth Montgomery (254 shows)
Serena	Elizabeth Montgomery (24)
Darrin Stephens #1 (1964-1969)	Dick York (156 shows)
Darrin Stephens #2 (1969-1972)	Dick Sargent (84)
Endora	Agnes Moorehead (147)
Larry Tate	David White (166 shows)
Louise Tate #1 (1964-1966)	Irene Vernon (13)
Louise Tate #2 (1966-1972)	Kasey Rogers (33)
Gladys Kravitz #1 (1964-1966)	Alice Pearce (28) [d. 3/66]
Gladys Kravitz #2 (1966-1972)	Sandra Gould (29)
Abner Kravitz	George Tobias (54)
Maurice	Maurice Evans (12)
Uncle Arthur (1965-1972)	Paul Lynde (10)
Doctor Bombay	Bernard Fox (18 shows)
Aunt Clara (1964-1968)	Marion Lorne (28 shows)
Tabitha Stephens (1966-1972)	Erin & Diane Murphy (100)
Frank Stephens #1 (1964-1967; 1971)	Robert F. Simon (6)
Frank Stephens #2 (1967-1970)	Roy Roberts (7)
Phyllis Stephens	Mabel Albertson (19)
Esmeralda (1969-1972)	Alice Ghostley (15)
Adam Stephens (1971-1972)	David & Greg Lawrence (17)

OCCASIONAL ROLES

Below is a listing of characters that were occasionally seen on *Bewitched*.

CHARACTERS	PLAYED BY
Aunt Enchantra	Estelle Winwood
Aunt Hepzibah	Jane Connel
Cousin Edgar	Arte Johnson
Cousin Henry	Steve Franken
Cousin Helen	Louise Glenn
Sidney Kravitz	Ricky Powell
Harriet Kravitz	Mary Grace Canfield
Jon Tate	Mitchell Silberman
Aunt Hagatha	Ysabel MacLosky (4 episodes)
	Reta Shaw (4 episode)
The Apothecary	Bernie Kopell
Betty, the secretary	Marcia Wallace
	Samantha Scott
	Jean Blake
The drunk at the bar	Dick Wilson (16 episodes)
Howard McMann	Leon Ames
	Gilbert Roland
Margaret McMann	Louise Sorel

BEWITCHED TECHNICAL CREDITS

Music: Warren Barker, Jimmie Haskell

Executive Producer: Harry Ackerman

Producer: William Froug, Danny Arnold, Jerry Davis, Danny Arnold, Jerry Davis

Director: William Asher (Directed 131 shows), Ernest Losso, Richard Michaels (Directed 54 shows), R. Robert Rosenbaum (22 shows), Jerry Davis (Directed 4 shows), Richard Kinon (9 shows), and E.W. Swackhamer (8 shows)
Note:
Ida Lupino directed #17, "*A is for Aardvark*".
David White directed #182, "*Samantha's Double Mother Trouble*".

Writers: Ed Jurist (wrote 51 shows, plus 2 as co-writer), Michael Morris (wrote 22 shows), Sol Saks, Danny Arnold, Bernard Slade (wrote 17 shows each), Ron Friedman, Howard Morris, John L. Greene & Paul David (wrote 8 a piece), James Henerson (wrote 10), Peggy Chandler, Douglas Tibbles, Lila Garrett& Bernie Kahn (wrote 10 shows), Rick Mittleman, Richard Baer (wrote 23 shows), Phillip & Henry Sharp, Ruth Brooks Flippen

Executive Producer: Harry Ackerman

Producer: William Asher, William Froug, Jerry Davis, Danny Arnold

Production Consultant: William Asher

Production Supervisor: Seymour Friedman

Post Production Supervisor: Lawrence Werner

Creator: Sol Saks

Production Company: Screen Gems Company

Syndication: Columbia Pictures TV

Associate Producer: Richard Michaels, Ernest Losso, Jerry Briskin

Director of Photography: Robert Tobey, Robert Wyckoff, Frederick Gately, Lloyd Ahern

Art Directors: Ross Bellan, Robert Purcell, Malcolm C. Bert, Robert Peterson

Film Editor : Aaron Nibley, Jack Ruggiero, Hugh Chaloupka, Jack Peluso, Asa Clark, Michael Luciano, Gerard J. Wilson, Bud Molin

Camera Operator: Val O'Malley

Casting: Ernest A. Losso, Sally Powers, Al Onorato, Burt Metcalfe

Set Decorator: Sidney Clifford, Louis Diage, Jack Ahern, Milton Stumph, James M. Crowe

Special Effects : Hal Bigger, Marlowe Newkirk, Richard Albain, Terry Saunders

Assistant Director : Maxwell Henry, R. Robert Rosenbaum, Mark Sandrich, Hal Polaire, Marvin Miller, Gil Mandelik, Jerome Siegel, Jack Orbison, Michael Dmytryk, Jack R. Berne, Anthony M. Ray, Dick Dixon

Music Effects: **Sunset** Editorial

HairStyles: Peanuts

Men's Costumes: Byron Munson

Ladies Costumes : Vi Alford

Title Song: **Howard** Greenfield, Jack Keller

Script Consultant: **Ruth** Brooks Flippen, Bernard Slade, and Danny Arnold

Music Consultant: Don Kirshner

Music Supervisor: Ed Forsyin

Makeup: Rolf Miller, Ben Lane

Make-up Supervisor: Ben Lane

Optical: Photo Effex

Production Secretary: Bobbi Shane

Sound Effects: Fred J. Brown, Sid Lubow, and Sunset Editorial

Dick York's Wardrobe: Michaels-Stern, Phoenix Clothes

Dick Sargent's Wardrobe: Botany 500, Michaels-Stern

Elizabeth Montgomery's Wardrobe: PFC Inc., York Town Juniors, Toni Lynn Maternities

Tabitha's (infant) Wardrobe & Furnishings: Babycrest

Props: George Ballerino

Camera Operator: Val O'Malley

Assistant to the Producer: Bobbi Shane

Production Secretary: Bobbi Shane

Gaffer: Arthur D. Kaufman

Property Master : George Ballerino

Head Grip : Charles Gibbs

Color by: Pathe, Perfect Pathe, Berkey Pathe

An Ashmont Production for Screen Gems

Trivia Tidbit:
Ashmont Productions is a combination of William Asher and Elizabeth Montgomery's two last names.

The Bewitched Movie Cast Credits

Trivia Tidbit:
Director and actress Penny Marshall originally
Shopped a Bewitched big screen script around Hollywood
In the early 1990's.

Trivia Tidbit:
Nicole Kidman and a friend were having a "Girl's Night In"
and the friend brought up Nicole's childhood
Fascination with Elizabeth Montgomery and her love of the television
Show Bewitched. The next day, Nicole called Sony Pictures and asked them
If they had a Bewitched project in the works. Immediately, the put a project together
And the Bewitched movie was born!

Plot Outline: A producer decides to remake the classic sitcom "Bewitched" and unknowingly casts a real witch in the lead role.

Bewitched Movie Release Date into theatres:	June 24, 2005
Writer	Delia and Nora Ephron
Director	Nora Ephron
Role	Played By
Isabel Bigelow/Samantha Stephens	Nicole Kidman
Jack Wyatt/Darrin Stephens	Will Ferrell
Iris Smythson/Endora	Shirley MacLaine
Nigel/Maurice type character	Michael Caine
Ritchie	Jason Schwartzman
Nina Johnson	Heather Burns
Maria Kelly	Sally Upland
Larry Tate	Jim Turner
Stu Robison	Stephen Colbert
Jim Fields	David Alan Grier
Uncle Arthur	Steve Carell
Pretty Model	Valerie Azlynn
Joey Props	Michael Badalucco
Francine Michaels	Roxanne Beckford
Press Conference Reporter	Sunday Boling
Press Conference Reporter	Bridget Ann Brno
Pete	P.J. Byrne
Writer #2	Ken Hudson Campbell
Auditioning Actress #15	Katie Carroll
Marie	Kristin Chenoweth
Reporter	Susan Chuang
Reporter	Kristi Clainos
Hillary	Julie Claire
Actress	Dawn Ashley Cook
Producer	Brian David
Cable Man	Jonathan T. Floyd
Victoria the waitress	Heather Freedman
Dinner Guest #6	Todd Hacker
Dinner Guest #3	Jennifer Haworth
Dinner Guest	Aidel D. Herrera
Photographer	Bryan Holly
Abner Kravitz	Richard Kind
	Nick Lachey
Electric #2	Tony Malanga
E! Anchor	Wendi McLendon-Covey
Quarreling Shopper	Annie Mumulo

RATINGS:

The following is where *Bewitched* fit in according to its standing in the over-all television sitcom ratings for each year.
*Percentage of TV viewers as ranked by Nielson.

> 254 Episodes (180 Color; 74 Black and White)
> First Telecast: September 17, 1964
> Last Telecast: July 1, 1972

Bewitching Fact: In 1964, with *Bewitched*'s 31.0 ranking, it was the highest season-long rating for an ABC sitcom until *Happy Days* surpassed it in 1977 with 31.5%.

> ABC Daytime January 1, 1968 to September 1973
> ABC Saturday Mornings 1971 to 1973
> Entered National Syndication September 1973 via Screen Gems
> Still in syndication through barter with Dancer Fitzgerald Sample of New York.

BROADCAST HISTORY:

September 1964-January 1967, ABC Thursday 9:00-9:30 PM
January 1967-September 1971, ABC Thursday 8:30-9:00 PM
September 1971-January 1972, ABC Wednesday 8:00-8:30 PM
January 1972-July 1972, ABC Saturday 8:00-8:30 PM

1964-1965
2. *Bewitched*
3. *Gomer Pyle*
4. *The Andy Griffith Show*
5. *The Dick Van Dyke Show*
8. *The Lucy Show*
12. *The Beverly Hillbillies*
13. *My Three Sons*
15. *Petticoat Junction*
18. *The Munsters*
19. *Gilligan's Island*
23. *The Addams Family*
24. *My Favorite Martian*

1965-1966
2. *Gomer Pyle*
3. *The Lucy Show*
6. *Andy Griffith Show*
7. **Bewitched**
8. *Beverly Hillbillies*
9. *Hogan's Heroes*
11. *Green Acres*
12. *Get Smart*
15. *My Three Sons*
16. *Dick Van Dyke Show*
21. *Petticoat Junction*
22. *Gilligan's Island*

1966-1967
3. *Andy Griffith Show*
4. *The Lucy Show*
6. *Green Acres*
8. **Bewitched**
9. *The Beverly Hillbillies*
10. *Gomer Pyle*
15. *Family Affair*
18. *Hogan's Heroes*
22. *Get Smart*
23. *Petticoat Junction*

1967-1968
1. *The Andy Griffith Show*
2. *The Lucy Show*
3. *Gomer Pyle*
5. *Family Affair*
11. **Bewitched**
12. *The Beverly Hillbillies*
16. *Green Acres*
24. *My Three Sons*

1968-1969
2. *Gomer Pyle*
4. *Mayberry, RFD*
5. *Family Affair*

7. *Julia*
9. *Here's Lucy*
10. *The Beverly Hillbillies*
12. **Bewitched**
14. *My Three Sons*
19. *Green Acres*

1969-1970
4. *Mayberry, RFD*
5. *Family Affair*
6. *Here's Lucy*
10. *The Doris Day Show*
11. *The Bill Cosby Show*
15. *My Three Sons*
18. *The Beverly Hillbillies*
25. **Bewitched**

1970-1971
Not In top Twenty-five

1971-1972
Not In top Twenty-five

Spin-off: **Tabitha**
Pilot: April 24, 1976 (*Tabatha*) & September 10, 1977

First Telecast: November 12, 1977
Last Telecast: August 25, 1978

Series History:
8:00 November 1977 to January 1978 Saturday
8:00 June to August 1978 Friday

Nick at Nite channel began showing black-and-white seasons of *Bewitched* in the Fall of 1989.

THE EMMYS: WHAT *BEWITCHED* WON

Bewitching Fact: Despite Agnes Moorehead's popularity and dedication to acting, she never received an Emmy (nominated six times). She also was not lucky in obtaining another type of achievement emblem, the Oscar, as she lost there also (was nominated five times).

It was surprising that *Bewitched* with an eight-year long duration on television only received 3 Emmy Awards, even though they were nominated 22 times. What was also surprising was that neither Agnes Moorehead nor Elizabeth Montgomery received an Emmy Award despite Moorehead being nominated six times, and Montgomery being nominated five times.

Emmy Awards
1965-1966

Alice Pearce (*Bewitched*)-Outstanding Performance by an Actress in a Supporting Role in a Comedy

William Asher (*Bewitched*)-Outstanding Directorial Achievement in a Comedy

1967-1968

Marion Lorne (*Bewitched*)-Outstanding Performance by an Actress in a Supporting Role in a Comedy

EMMY NOMINATIONS
1965/1966
Presented May 22, 1966

Outstanding Comedy Series
  Dick Van Dyke Show (CBS)
  Batman (ABC)
  Bewitched (ABC)
  Get Smart (NBC)
  Hogan's Heroes (CBS)

Outstanding Continued Performance By An Actress In A Leading Role In A Comedy Series
    *Mary Tyler *Moore, Dick Van Dyke Show* (CBS)
    Lucille Ball, *The Lucy Show* (CBS)
    Elizabeth Montgomery, *Bewitched* (ABC)

Outstanding Performance By An Actress In A Supporting Role In A Comedy
    *Alice Pearce, *Bewitched* (ABC)
    Agnes Moorehead, *Bewitched* (ABC)
    Rose Marie, *Dick Van Dyke Show* (CBS)

Outstanding Directorial Achievement In A Comedy
    *William Asher, *Bewitched* (ABC)
    Paul Bogart, *Get Smart* (NBC)
    Jerry Paris, *Dick Van Dyke Show* (CBS)

1966/1967
Presented June 4, 1967

Outstanding Comedy Series
    **The Monkees* (NBC)*
    Bewitched (ABC)
    Get Smart (NBC)
    Andy Griffith Show (CBS)
    Hogan's Heroes (CBS)

Outstanding Continued Performance By An Actress In A Leading Role In A Comedy Series
    Elizabeth Montgomery, *Bewitched* (ABC)
    Agnes Moorehead, *Bewitched* (ABC)
    *Lucille Ball, *The Lucy Show* (CBS)
    Marlo Thomas, *That Girl* (ABC)

Outstanding Performance By An Actress In A Supporting Role In A Comedy
    Marion Lorne, *Bewitched* (ABC)
    *Frances Bavier, *The Andy Griffith Show* (CBS)
    Nancy Kulp, *The Beverly Hillbillies* (CBS)

Outstanding Directorial Achievement In A Comedy
   William Asher, *Bewitched* (ABC)
   *James Frawley, The Monkees (NBC)

1967/1968
Presented May 19, 1968

Outstanding Comedy Series
   **Get Smart* (NBC)
   Bewitched (ABC)
   Family Affair (CBS)
   Hogan's Heroes (CBS)
   Lucy Show (CBS)

Outstanding Continued Performance By An Actor In A Leading Role In A Comedy Series
   *Don Adams, *Get Smart* (NBC)
   Richard Benjamin, *He and She* (CBS)
   Sebastian Cabot, *Family Affair* (CBS)
   Brian Keith, *Family Affair* (CBS)
   Dick York, *Bewitched* (ABC)

Outstanding Continued Performance By An Actress In A Leading Role In A Comedy Series
   *Lucille Ball, *The Lucy Show*, (CBS)
   Barbara Feldon, *Get Smart* (NBC)
   Elizabeth Montgomery, *Bewitched* (ABC)

Outstanding Performance By An Actress In A Supporting Role In A Comedy
   *Marion Lorne, *Bewitched* (ABC)
   Agnes Moorehead, *Bewitched* (ABC)
   Marge Redmond, *The Flying Nun* (ABC)
   Nita Talbot, *Hogan's* Heroes (CBS)

1968/1969
Presented June 8, 1969

Outstanding Comedy Series
   **Get Smart* (CBS)
   Bewitched (ABC)

Family Affair (CBS)
The Ghost and Mrs. Muir (NBC)
Julia (NBC)

Outstanding Continued Performance By An Actress In A Leading Role In A Comedy
  *Hope Lange, *The Ghost and Mrs. Muir* (NBC)
  Diahann Carroll, *Julia* (NBC)
  Barbara Feldon, *Get Smart* (NBC)
  Elizabeth Montgomery, *Bewitched* (ABC)

Outstanding Continued Performance By An Actress In A Supporting Role In A Series
  *Susan Saint James, *The Name of the Game* (NBC)
  Barbara Anderson, *Ironside* (NBC)
  Agnes Moorehead, *Bewitched* (ABC)

1969/1970
Presented June 7, 1970

Outstanding Continued Performance By An Actress In A Leading Role In A Comedy Series
  *Hope Lange, *The Ghost and Mrs. Muir* (NBC)
  Elizabeth Montgomery, *Bewitched* (ABC)
  Marlo Thomas, *That Girl* (ABC)

Outstanding Performance By An Actress In A Supporting Role In A Comedy
  *Karen Valentine, *Room 222* (ABC)
  Agnes Moorehead, *Bewitched* (ABC)
  Lurene Tuttle, *Julia* (NBC)

1970/1971
Outstanding Performance By An Actress In A Supporting Role In A Comedy
  *Valerie Harper, *The Mary Tyler Moore Show* (CBS)
  Agnes Moorehead, *Bewitched* (ABC)
  Karen Valentine, *Room 222 (ABC)*

Outstanding Achievement In Make-Up
  *Robert Dawn, "Catafalque", *Mission: Impossible* (CBS)
  Marie Roche, "Hamlet", *Hallmark Hall of Fame* (NBC)

Rolf J. Miller, "Samantha's Old Man", *Bewitched* (ABC)
Perc Westmore, Harry C. Blake, *The Third Bill Cosby Show* (NBC)

1971/1972
None

*Denotes Winner

BEWITCHING REMAKES AND SEMI-REMAKES

The following is a listing of *Bewitched* remakes and semi-remakes with either identical or similar storylines: Often times, a popular storyline from an earlier season would get rewritten, reinvented, and shifted slightly. Many times, in my opinion, the second version would not be as effective since it wasn't exactly an original. Other networks too, with an adversarial television product, like I Dream of Jeannie, would have their writers work up similar storylines for their characters as well.

Episode	Name of Episode
3	It Shouldn't Happen to a Dog *
196	A Chance on Love
5	Help, Help Don't Save Me *
252	A Good Turn Never Goes Unpunished
6	Little Pitches Have Big Fears
90	Soapbox Derby
8	The Girl Reporter
194	Generation Zap
11	It Takes One to Know One *
240	Eight Year Itch Witch
23	Red Light, Green Light
34	Remember The Main
27	There's No Witch Like An Old Witch *
243	Samantha's Magic Sitter

29	Abner Kadabra *
228	Samantha and the Antique Doll
32	Illegal Separation
140	Splitsville
37	Alias Darrin Stephens
222	Darrin Goes Ape
39	We're In For A Bad Spell *
179	Samantha's Secret Spell
42 *	Take Two Aspirins and Half of Pint of Porpoise Milk
253	Samantha's Witchcraft Blows a Fuse
46	Junior Executive *
224	Out of the Mouths of Babes
47	Aunt Clara's Old Flame *
226	Samantha's Magic Mirror
50	Speak The Truth *
254	The Truth, Nothing but the Truth, So Help Me, Sam
69	Divided He Falls *
185	Samantha's Better Halves
87-88	My Friend Ben/Samantha For The Defense
249-50	George Washington Zapped Here 1 & 2
143	Samantha On the Keyboard
246	Samantha On Thin Ice
196	A Chance On Love
245	Serena's Richcraft

* Denotes almost direct remake
The Episodes—#50/254 is the most obvious remake in the series.

I DREAM OF JEANNIE SIMILAR STORYLINE

Here are just a few *I Dream of Jeannie* episodes that are similar to *Bewitched* episodes.

Episode	Name of Episode
18	The Cat's Meow (Bewitched)
6	The Yacht Murder Case (I Dream of Jeannie)
80	Endora Moves in for a Spell (Bewitched)
81	Twitch or Treat (Bewitched)
14	What House Across the Street? (I Dream of Jeannie)
69	Divided He Falls
185	Samantha's Better Halves
15	Too Many Tony's (I Dream of Jeannie)
98	Art For Sam's Sake (Bewitched)
26	My Master, the Great Rembrandt (I Dream of Jeannie)
114	Birdies, Bogeys and Baxter (Bewitched)
23	Watch the Birdie (I Dream of Jeannie)
125	Once in a Vial (Bewitched)
30	I'll Never Forget What's Her Name (I Dream of Jeannie)

SHOWS DICK YORK MISSED

Dick York injured his back while filming the 1959 Western, They Came to Cordura. This left Mr. York in constant pain. According to some of the regular cast members, some mornings his pain was so great, that he was unable to show up to work in the morning. When Mr. York was able to make it to a shoot, but was not feeling well, William Asher used his creativity to help alleviate Mr. York's pain. In some episodes, one can see Dick York laying on the Stephens' couch, or sitting in a chair at breakfast, or simply remaining seated in his office chair at McMann & Tate.

DATE	EPISODE	NAME OF EPISODE
12-22-66	No. 89	*A Gazebo Never Forgets*
3-9-67	No. 100	*Aunt Clara's Victor Victoria*
2-8-68	No. 129	*A Prince of a Guy*
3-21-68	No. 133	*Playmates*
3-28-68	No. 134	*Tabitha's Cranky Spell*
4-11-68	No. 136	*A Majority of Two*
2-13-69	No. 160	*Mrs. Stephens, Where Are You?*
2-20-69	No. 161	*Marriage, Witches Style*
2-27-69	No. 162	*Going Ape*
3-6-69	No. 163	*Tabitha's Weekend*
3-20-69	No. 165	*Samantha's Power Failure*
3-27-69	No. 166	*Samantha Twitches for UNICEF*
4-10-69	No. 168	*Samantha's Good News*
4-17-69	No. 169	*Samantha's Shopping Spree*

REGULARS ONLY

The following is a listing of episodes in which only regular cast members and/or semi-regular cast members were featured.

Trivia Tidbit:
Kasey Rogers, also known as the second Louise Tate,
Brought many of the outfits that she wore on
Bewitched from her own closet.

Episode	Episode Name	Cast Members
NO. 2	"Be it Ever So Mortgaged"	Sam, Darrin, Endora, Abner, Gladys
NO. 14	"Samantha Meets the Folks"	Sam, Darrin, Phyllis, Frank
NO. 17	"A Is For Aardvark"	Sam, Darrin, Endora Larry
NO. 29	"Abner Kadabra"	Sam, Darrin, Abner, Gladys
NO. 37	"Alias Darrin Stephens"	Sam, Darrin, Endora, Larry, Clara, Abner, Gladys
NO. 56	"Samantha Meets the Folks" (recut version of #14)	Sam, Darrin, Phyllis, Frank
NO. 72	"What Every Young Man Should Know"	Sam, Darrin, Endora, Larry
NO. 76	"Moment of Truth"	Sam, Darrin, Larry, Clara, Louise, Tabitha
NO. 78	"Accidental Twins"	Sam, Darrin, Larry, Clara, Louise, Tabitha
NO. 116	"Out of Sync, Out of Mind"	Sam, Darrin, Clara, Frank, Phyllis, Bombay
NO. 150	"Samantha Loses Her Voice"	Sam, Darrin, Arthur, Larry, Louise, Tabitha
NO. 163	"Tabitha's Weekend"	Sam, Endora, Phyllis, Frank, Tabitha
NO. 176	"Naming Samantha's New Baby"	Sam, Darrin, Endora, Maurice, Frank, Phyllis, Tabitha
NO. 195	"Okay, Who's the Wise Witch?"	Sam, Darrin, Endora, Larry, Bombay, Tabitha, Esmeralda
NO. 198	"Mona Sammy"	Sam, Darrin, Endora, Larry, Louise
NO. 228	"Samantha and the Antique Doll"	Sam, Darrin, Phyllis, Frank, Adam

TELEVISION AND FILM CREDITS
Elizabeth Montgomery as Samantha Stephens

<u>Movie Credits:</u>
The Court Martial of Billy Mitchell, 1955
Who's Been Sleeping in my Bed?, 1963
Johnny Cool, 1963
The Victim, 1972
A Case of Rape, 1974
The Legend of Lizzie Borden, 1975
Dark Victory, 1976
A Killing Affair, 1977
The Awakening Land, 1978
Jennifer: A Woman's Story, 1979
Act of Violence, 1980
Belle Star, 1981
When the Circus Came to Town, 1982
The Rules of Marriage, 1983
Second Sight: A Love Story, 1985
Sins of a Mother, 1991
Black Widow Murder: The Blanche Taylor Moore Story, 1993

Alocoa Premiere
Alfred Hitchcock Presents
Armstrong Circle Theatre
Dupont Show of the Month
Kraft Theatre
Robert Montgomery Presents
Studio One
Tab Hunter Show
Twilight Zone
Untouchables

<u>Dick York as Darrin Stephens (Darrin #1)</u>

<u>Movie Credits:</u>
Three Stripes in the Sun
My sister Eileen
Operation Mad Ball

They Came to Cordura
Cowboy
Inherit the Wind

TV Series and Appearances:
Alcoa Theatre
Alfred Hitchcock Presents
Climax
Dr. Kildare
Father Knows Best
Going My Way
Goodyear Playhouse
Justice
Kaiser Aluminum Hour
Kraft Theatre
Philco Playhouse
Playwrights '56
Playhouse 90
Rawhide
Studio One
The Millionaire
Twilight Zone
Twilight Zone
U.S. Steel Hour
Untouchables
Wagon Train

Darrin Stephens (Darrin #2)

Film Credits:
Bernardine, 1959
Mardi Gras
Operation Petticoat
That Touch of Mink
Captain Newman, M.D.
The Ghost and Mr. Chicken
The Private Navy of Sgt. O'Farrell
Hardcore
Body Count
Teen Witch
Rock-a-Die-Baby

TV Series and Appearances:
Melvin Purvis
G-Man
Fantasy Island (pilot)
The Power Within
The Gossip Columnist
Taxi
One Happy Family
Broadside
The Tammy Grimes Show

Agnes Moorehead as Endora

Film Credits:
Citizen Kane, 1941
The Magnificent Ambersons, 1942
Government Girl, 1943
Mrs. Parkington, 1944
Our Vines Have Tender Grapes, 1945
Dark Passage, 1947
Johnny Belinda, 1948
Show Boat, 1951
Untamed, 1955
Pollyanna, 1960
Bachelor in Paradise, 1961
Hush, Hush, Sweet Charlotte, 1964

TV Credits and Appearances:
Alcoa Theatre
The Best In Mystery
The Chevy Mystery Show
Revelon Mirror Theatre
The Twilight Zone
Shirley Temple's Storybook

David White as Larry Tate

Film Credits:

Sweet Smell of Success, 1957
The Apartment, 1960

Sunrise at Campobello, 1960
The Great Impostor, 1961
Madison Avenue, 1962

Television Series and Appearances:
The Betty Hutton Show
The Slightly Fallen Angel
Spider-Man
Twin Detectives
The Rockford Files
Rhoda
Kraft Theatre
The Untouchables
Cagney and Lacey

Marion Lorne as Aunt Clara

Trivia Tidbit:
Marion Lorne was named Aunt Clara in the 1955 Rosalind Russell musical, *The Girl Rush*.

Movie Credits:
Strangers on a Train, 1951
The Girl Rush, 1955
The Graduate, 1968

Television Series and Appearances:
Dupont Show of the Month
The Gary Moore Show
The Ed Sullivan Show
The Dinah Shore Show
The Jack Paar Show
Mr. Peppers
Sally, 1957
Suspicion

Alice Pearce as Gladys Kravitz (Gladys #1)

Film Credits:
The Belle of New York, 1952

How to Be Very Very Popular, 1955
The Opposite Sex, 1956
My Six Loves, 1963
Tammy and the Doctor, 1963
Lad: A Dog, 1962
The Thrill of It All, 1963
Bus Riley's Back In Town, 1965
The Glass Bottom Boat, 1966

TV Credits:
Jamie
One Minute Please

Sandra Gould as Gladys Kravitz (Gladys #2)

TV Series and Appearances:
I Married Joan
TV Funnies
December Bride
I Dream of Jeannie
I Love Lucy
The Danny Thomas Show
Tabitha

George Tobias as Abner Kravitz

Movie Credits:
Saturday's Children (debut), 1940
City For Conquest, 1940
Sergeant York, 1941
Yankee Doodle Dandy, 1942
This is the Army, 1943
Thank Your Lucky Stars, 1943
Between Two Worlds, 1944
Objective Burma, 1945
Mildred Pierce, 1945
Sinbad the Sailor, 1947
Rawhide, 1950
The Glenn Miller Story, 1953
The Seven Little Foys, 1955

A New kind of Love, 1963
The Glass Bottom Boat, 1966

<u>TV Series and Appearances</u>:
Adventures in Paradise
Hudson's Bay
Telephone Time
Tabitha
The Waltons

Alice Ghostley as Esmeralda

<u>Movie Credits:</u>
New Faces, 1954
To Kill a Mockingbird, 1962
My Six Loves, 1963
The Flim Flam Man, 1967
Viva Max, 1968
Ace Eli and Rodger of the Skies, 1972

<u>TV Series and Appearances:</u>
Cross-Wits
Designing Women
The Jackie Gleason Show
The Jonathan Winters Show
The Julie Andrews Hour
Mayberry R.F.D.
Nichols
Temperatures Rising

Maurice Evans as Maurice

<u>Film Credits:</u>
White Cargo, 1930
Raise the Roof, 1930
Should a Doctor Tell?, 1930
Wedding Rehearsal, 1932
Scrooge, 1935
Kind Lady, 1951
Androcles and the Lion, 1953

Gilbert and Sullivan, 1953
The War Lord, 1965
Jack of Diamonds, 1967
Planet of the Apes, 1968
Rosemary's Baby, 1968
The Body Stealers, 1970
Beneath the Planet of the Apes, 1970
Terror in the Wax Museum, 1973

Television Series and Appearances:
I Spy
Batman
The Mod Squad
Search
Macbeth
Richard II
The Taming of the Shrew
Twelfth Night
Man and Superman
Caesar and Cleopatra

Bernard Fox as Dr. Bombay

Movie Credits:
Star of India, 1954
The Safecracker, 1958

TV Series and Appearances:
*Tabitha (Bewitched spin-off)
The Andy Griffith Show
General Hospital
Hogan's Heroes
Intertect
Make Room for Daddy
Sherlock Holmes: The Hound of Baskervilles
Soap
The Son-In-Law
The Wide Open Door

Paul Lynde as Uncle Arthur

Film Credits:
New Faces, 1954
Son of Flubber, 1963
Under the Yum Yum Tree, 1963
Bye Bye Birdie, 1963
For Those Who Think Young, 1964
Send Me No Flowers, 1964
Beach Blanket Bingo, 1965
The Glass Bottom Boat, 1966
How Sweet It Is, 1968
Charlotte's Web (voice only), 1973
Journey Back to Oz (voice only), 1974
Hugo the Hippo (voice only), 1976
The Villain, 1978

TV Series and Appearances
Dean Martin Presents
Donny and Marie Show
Hey Landlord
Hollywood Squares
Love, American Style
Stanley
Temperature's Rising
The Jonathan Winters Show
The Paul Lynde Show
The Pruitt's of Southampton

Mabel Albertson as Phyllis Stephens

Movie Credits:
Mutiny on the Blackhawk, 1939
She's back on Broadway, 1953
Ransom, 1956
Forever Darling, 1956
The Long Hot Summer, 1958
Home Before Dark, 1958
The Gazebo, 1960
Period of Adjustment, 1962

Barefoot in the Park, 1967
On a Clear day, you can see Forever, 1970
What's Up Doc, 1972

TV Appearances and Credits:
That's My Boy
Those Whiting Girls
The Tom Ewell Show

Robert F. Simon as Frank Stephen (Mr. Stephens #1)
Movie Credits:

TV Appearances:
Amazing Spider-Man
Broken Arrow
El Fego Baca
The Girl in the Empty Grawl
The Legend of Custer
Nancy Saints and Sinners
The Six Million Dollar Man
The Web

Roy Roberts as Frank Stephens (Mr. Stephens #2)

Trivia Tidbit:
Robert (Roy) F. Simons also appeared in Elizabeth Montgomery's first movie, *The Court Martial of Billy Mitchell*, Warner Brothers, 1955.

Movie Credits:
Guadalcanal Diary, 1943
My Darling Clementine, 1946
Flaming Fury, 1949
The Big Trees, 1952
The Glory Brigade, 1953
The Court Martial of Billy Mitchell
The Boss, 1956
Hotel

TV Appearances:
Petticoat Junction
The Lucy Show
The Gale Storm Show

Irene Vernon as Louise Tate (Mrs. Tate #1)

Movie Credits:
Do Not Disturb
Fireside Theater

Kasey Rogers as Louise Tate (Mrs. Tate #2)

Movie Credits:
Silver City, 1951
Stranger on a Train, 1951
Denver and Rio Grande, 1952
Jamaica Rum, 1953

TV Credits:
Peyton Place

Richard Michaels (Director/Producer)

Television Shows:
Big Hawaii
The Brady Bunch
Delvechio
The Flying Num
Jessie
Kelly's Kids
Once an Eagle
Room 222

William Asher (Director/Producer)

Television Shows:
Tabitha (Bewitched spin-off)
Alice
Bad News Bears

Charley's Aunt
A Christmas for Boomer
Crazy like a Fox
The Dukes of Hazzard
Flatbust
Gidget
Harper Valley
Harper Valley PTA
Temperature's Rising
Private Benjamin
The Paul Lynde Show
Operation Petticoat

Film Credits:
Leather Gloves, 1948
The Shadow on the Window, 1957
The 27th Day, 1957
Beach Party, 1963
Johnny Cool, 1963
Muscle Beach Party, 1964
Bikini Beach, 1964
How to Stuff a Wild Bikini, 1965
Fireball 500, 1966

Sol Saks (Creator of Pilot)

TV Movie Credits:
An Apartment In Rome, 1964 (writer and producer)
Out of the Blue, 1968 (writer and producer)

Danny Arnold (Producer)

Television Series and Movies:
Barney Miller (Creator with Theodore Flicker)
My World ... and Welcome to It
The Real McCoys, 1962 (Producer and story editor)
Somewhere In Italy
Company B
Tennessee Ernie Ford Show (Writer)
Rosemary Clooney Show, 1956 (Writer)

That Girl, 1967-69 (Producer)
Stat, 1990-91 (Executive Producer)

Harry Ackerman (Executive Producer)

Television Credits:
All in the Family
Dennis the Menace
The Eve Arden Show
The Flying Nun
Gidget
Gidget Gets Married
Gidget's Summer Reunion
Hazel
Leave it to Beaver
My sister Eileen
The Paul Lynde Show
Temperatures Rising
Bachelor Father
The Farmer's Daughter

BEWITCHED ESTIMATED COST PER EPISODE:
   1964-1966 $80,000 PER EPISODE
   1971-1972 $115,000 PER EPISODE.

BEWITCHED EPISODES
   There are 254 Episodes of *Bewitched*.
   There is one *Bewitched* episode held in the Library of Congress and it is the "Solid Gold Mother-In Law" episode.

Samantha is a beautiful witch and the wife of Manhattan Advertising executive Darrin Stephens.

First Season
September 1964 to June 1965

Sam and Darrin met going through a revolving door at the Clark Building in New York City (#1).

No. 1 _____

I, Darrin, Take This Witch Samantha (Pilot) 9/17/64
GS: Nancy Kovack as Sheila, Gene Blakely as Dave, Lindsay Workman as the doctor, and Paul Barselow as the bartender. Writer: Sol Saks. Directed by: William Asher.
After they are married, Samantha tells Darrin that she is a Witch.

Bewitching Fact:
In the original pilot script the character names were Darrin and Cassandra Douglas.

No. 2 _____

Be It ever So Mortgaged 9/24/64
Writer: Barbara Avedon. Directed by: William Asher
Samantha tries to prove to her mother that her new house is a nice place to live.
"We are quicksilver, a fleeting shadow, a distant sound. Our home has no boundaries beyond which we cannot pass. We live in music, in a flash of color. We live on the wind and
In the Sparkle of a star."-Endora

No. 3 _____

It Shouldn't Happen To a Dog 10/1/64
GS: Jack Warden as Rex Barker, Grace Lee Whitney as Babs Livingston, Monroe Arnold as Dr. Jackson, Karl Lukas as the first policeman. Writer: Jerry Davis.
Directed by: William Asher.
Samantha turns one of Darrin's clients into a dog.

What is the name of Darrin's client in episode #3, "It Shouldn't To A Dog?"
    A. Rex Barker
    B. Wink Martindale
    C. Kats McKenzie

What breed of dog does he become?

Who turns him into a dog?
    A. Serena
    B. Samantha
    C. Endora

Why was he turned into a dog?
    A. because of his attitude
    B. because he is a flirt
    C. because he likes dogs

Answers:
No. 4 _____

Mother, Meet What's His Name 10/08/64
GS: Alice Backes as June Foster, Hollis Irving as Shirley Clyde, John Copage at the phone repairman. Writer: Danny Arnold. Directed by: William Asher.
Samantha introduces Darrin to her mother for the first time.

No. 5 _____

Help, Help, Don't Save Me 10/15/64
GS: Charles Ruggles as Philip Caldwell. Writer: Danny Arnold. Directed by: William Asher.
Darrin accuses Samantha of using her witchcraft to ruin his ad campaign for a soup company.

No. 6 _____

Little Pitchers Have Big Fears 10/22/64
GS: June Lockhart as Mrs. Burns, Jerry Mathers as Marshall Burns, Byron Keith as Coach Gribben, Joel Davison as Floyd Kravitz, Art Lewis as the brush salesman, Joe Brooks as the umpire, Greger Vigen as the player. Writer: Barbara Avedon. Directed by: William Asher.
Samantha helps a boy with an overprotective mother play baseball.

No. 7_____

The Witches Are Out 10/29/64
GS: Shelley Berman as Brinkman, Madge Blake as Mary,
Reta Shaw as Bertha, Jacques Roux as the French Legionnaire.
Writer: Bernard Slade. Directed by: William Asher.
Samantha and some other witches try to convince Darrin's client to change the trademark on his Halloween candy from an ugly witch to a beautiful witch.

No. 8_____

The Girl Reporter 11/5/64
GS: Roger Ewing as Marvin "Monster" Grogan, Cheryl Holdridge as Liza Randall, Alex Gerry as Mr. Austen. Writers: Paul David and John L. Greene. Directed by: William Asher.
Darrin is interviewed by a girl reporter who has a jealous boyfriend.

No. 9_____

Witch or Wife 11/12/64
GS: Raquel Welch as the stewardess, Peter Camlin as the
waiter, Jon Coons as the man, Rowena Burack as the woman on
the plane. Writer: Bernard Slade. Directed by: William Asher.
Darrin believes that his marriage to Samantha is a mistake,
when he finds that, she followed him to Paris instead of
staying home where he believes she belongs.

No. 10_____

Just One Happy Family 11/19/64
GS: Thomas Anthony as the first customer, Charlie Dugdale as the second customer. Writers: Fred Freeman and Lawrence J. Cohen. Directed by: William Asher.
Samantha's father comes for a visit, unaware that Samantha has married a mortal.

No. 11_____

It Takes One To Know One 11/26/64
GS: Lisa Seagram as Jannine, Robert Cleaves as the photographer. Writer: Jack Sher. Directed by: William Asher.
Endora sends a beautiful witch to tempt Darrin away from Samantha.

No. 12_____

... And Something Makes Three 12/3/64
Writer: Danny Arnold. Directed by: William Asher.
Larry thinks Samantha is going to have a baby, unaware that it is his own wife that is pregnant.

No. 13_____

Love Is Blind 12/10/64
GS: Adam West as Kermit, Kit Smythe as Gertrude, Ralph Barnard as the minister, Chris Noel as Susan. Writer: Roland Wolpert. Directed by: William Asher.
Samantha tries to get her friend an artist to marry.

No. 14_____

Samantha Meets the Folks 12/17/64
Writer: Bernard Slade. Directed by: William Asher.
Darrin is worried that Samantha's Aunt Clara will ruin his parents' visit.

No. 15_____

A Vision of Sugar Plums 12/24/64
GS: Billy Mumy as Michael, Cecil Kellaway as Santa, Sara Seegar as Mrs. Grange, Kevin Tate as Tommy, Harry Monty as the dwarf, Gerry Johnson as Mrs. Johnson, Bill Daily as Mr. Johnson. Writer: Herman Groves. Directed by: William Asher.
Samantha tries to prove to a visiting orphan that Santa Claus really exists.

No. 16

It's Magic 1/7/65
GS: Walter Burke as Zeno, Cliff Norton as Norman the waiter, Virginia Martin as Roxie Ames, Alice Backes as June Foster, Hollis Irving as Shirley Clyde. Writers: Tom and Frank Waldman. Directed by: Sidney Miller.
Samantha helps a broken down magician regain his confidence.

No. 17

A Is for Aardvark 1/14/65
Writer: Earl Barret. Directed by: Ida Lupino.
When Darrin sprains his ankle and is confined to bed, Samantha gives him the power of witchcraft.

No. 18

The Cat's Meow 1/21/65
GS: Martha Hyer as Margaret Marshall, George Ives as Captain Kelly, Clarence Lung as Kujo, Harry Holcombe as Charlie Godfrey. Writers: Richard and Mary Sale. Directed by: David McDearmon.
Darrin visits an attractive businesswoman on her yacht and suspects that the cat that he finds might be Samantha checking up on him.

No. 19

A Nice Little Dinner Party 1/28/65
GS: Lindsay Workman as conductor, David Garner as the captain, Hap Holmwood as the co-pilot. Writer: Bernard Slade. Directed by: Sherman Marks.
Darrin's father falls for Endora.

No. 20

Your Witch Is Showing 2/4/65
GS: Jonathan Daily as Gideon Whitsett, Peggy Lipton as the secretary, Alex Gerrry as Mr. Woolfe. Writer: Joanne Lee.

Directed by: Joseph Pevney.
Darrin's new assistant steals his ideas in order to get Darrin's job for himself.

No. 21

Ling Ling 2/11/65
GS: Greta Chi as Ling Ling, Jeremy Slate as Walter Ames.
Writer: Jerry Davis. Directed by: David McDearmon.
Samantha turns their pet cat into an oriental girl so she can be the model for Darrin's ad campaign.

What is the name of the pet that Sam turns into an oriental girl?
   A. Sing Sing
   B. Ling
   C. Ding a Ling

What type of pet is the oriental girl?
   A. Dog
   B. Fish
   C. Cat

   Answers: B. Ling Ling; C. Cat

No. 22_____

Eye of the Beholder 2/25/65
GS: Peter Brocco as Mr. Bodkin, Gene Blakely as Dave, Mark Tapscott as Officer Kern, Paul Barselow as the bartender, Lindsay Workman as the doctor, Carter DeHaven as Henry, Georgia Schmidt as Agatha, Stephen Whittaker as Eddy, Cindy Eilbacher as Kimmie, Sharon DeBord as Miss Blanding. Writer: Herman Groves. Director: William Asher. Endora makes Darrin think Samantha will remain eternally young, while he grows old.

No. 23_____

Red Light, Green Light 3/4/65
GS: Gene Blakely as Joe Harvey, Dan Tobin as the mayor, Vic Tayback as the chauffeur, Robert Dorman as the policeman. Writer: Roland Wolper. Directed by: David McDearmon.
Samantha tries to convince the mayor that a traffic signal is needed on their block.

No. 24_____

Which Witch Is Witch? 3/11/65
GS: Ron Randell as Bob Frazer, Monty Margetts as the saleswoman, Donald Foster as the elderly gentleman. Writer: Earl Barret. Directed by: William D. Russell.
Endora transforms herself into an identical copy of Samantha, which causes problems when a young author falls for her.

No. 25_____

Pleasure O'Riley 3/18/65
GS: Kipp Hamilton as Pleasure O'Riley, Ken Scott as
Thor Swenson, William Woodson as the police sergeant,
Norman Burton as the moving man. Writer: Ken Englund.
Directed by: William D. Russell.
Darrin and Mr. Kravitz fall for a beautiful model that moves into the neighborhood,
unaware that she has a jealous boyfriend.

Episode #25
What is Pleasures' real name?
  A. Pricilla
  B. Penelope
  C. Patty

Episode #25
What does Pleasure have a lot of?
  A. Money
  B. Debt
  C. Ex-fiancées

Episode #25
What is Pleasures' profession?
  A. Model
  B. Actress
  C. Stewardess

Answers: A. Pricilla; C. Ex-fiancées; A. Model

No. 26_____

Driving Is the Only Way to Fly 3/25/65
GS: Paul Lynde as Harold, Paul Bryar as Basil Koenig.
Writer: Richard Baer. Directed by: William Asher.
Samantha takes driving lessons from a very nervous instructor.

No. 27

There's No Witch Like an Old Witch 4/1/65
GS: Reta Shaw as Bertha, Brian Nash as Jimmy Caldwell, Gilbert Green as Judge Virgil Winner, Karen Norris as Agnes Bain, Peg Shirley as Beatrice Caldwell, Michael Blake as Gary Bain, Vickie Malkin as Louise Bain, Nina Roman as Beulah, Penny Kunard as Shirley. Writers: Ted Sherdeman and Jane Klove. Directed by: William Asher.
Aunt Clara becomes a babysitter but causes trouble when she tells the children she looks after that she is a witch.

No. 28

Open the Door, Witchcraft 4/8/65
GS: Hal Bokar as Noel, Baynes Barron as Max, Eddie Hanley as the salesman. Writer: Ruth Brooks Flippen. Directed by: William Asher.
The Stephen's new electric garage door opener is affected by passing jets, causing it to open and close constantly.

No. 29_____

Abner Kadabra 4/15/65
Writers: Lawrence J. Cohen and Fred Freeman. Directed by: William Asher.
Samantha makes Mrs. Kravitz think she has ESP and magical powers.

No. 30_____

George the Warlock 4/22/65
GS: Christopher George as George, Beverly Adams as D.D. O'Riley, Lauren Gilbert as Porterfield, Sharon DeBord as Miss Thatcher. Writer: Ken Englund. Directed by: William Asher.
Endora gets a warlock to romance Samantha in order to break up her marriage to Darrin.

No. 31_____

That Was My Wife 4/29/65
GS: Warren Ott as Ellen. Writer: Bernard Slade. Directed by: William Asher.
Larry thinks Darrin is fooling around with another woman, unaware that it was really Samantha wearing a wig.

No. 32_____

Illegal Separation 5/6/65
GS: Dick Balduzzi as the salesman. Writer: Richard Baer. Directed by: William Asher.
Abner and Gladys Kravitz have a fight and he moves in with the Stephens's.

No. 33_____

A Change of Face 5/13/65
GS: Gene Blakely as Dave, Marily Hanold as Michelle, Elisa Ingram as Barbara Lucas, Henry Hunter as the doctor, Paul Barselow as the bartender, Dick Wilson as

the man in the bar. Writer: Bernard Slade. Directed by: William Asher.
Endora changes the features of Darrin's face in order to improve him.

No. 34_____

Remember the Main 5/20/65
GS: Byron Morrow as Hohn C. Cavanaugh, Justin Smith as Merrill Sedgwick, Edward Mallory as Ed Wright, Stuart Nesbit as Charles Turner. Writer: Mort R. Lewis. Directed by: William D. Russell.
Darrin blames Samantha for getting him involved in politics.

No. 35_____

Eat at Mario's 5/27/65
GS: Alan Hewitt as Baldwin, Vito Scotty as Mario, Phil Arnold as the vendor, Michael Quinn as the emcee. Writer: Richard Baer. Directed by: William Asher.
Samantha and Endora try to help publicize a restaurant at the expense of one of Darrin's clients.

No. 36_____

Cousin Edgar 6/3/65
GS: Arte Johnson as Edgar, Charles Irving as Shelley, Roy Stuart as Fred Froug. Writer: Paul Wayne. Directed by: E. W. Swackhamer.
Endora gets Samantha's cousin Edgar, an elf, to break up her daughter's marriage.

Bewitching Facts
There were 36 episodes of Bewitched in the first season. They were shown from 9-17-64 through 6-3-65, with no preemptions and only two reruns.

Second Season
September 1965 to June 1966

No. 37_____

Alias Darrin Stephens 9/16/65
Writer: Richard Baer. Directed by: William Asher.
Aunt Clara accidentally turns Darrin into a chimp.

No. 38_____

A Very Special Delivery 9/23/65
GS: Richard Vath as Phil, Henry Hunter as the doctor, John Graham as Martin, Gene Blakely as Dave, Dort Clark as the man in the bar. Writer: Howard Leeds. Directed by: William Asher.
Samantha tells Darrin that she is pregnant, which makes him very nervous.

No. 39_____

We're in for a Bad Spell 9/30/65
GS: William Redfield as Adam Newlarkin, William Tregoe as Mr. Peterson, Bartlett Robinson as Mr. Abercrombie, Richard X. Slattery as the detective, Arthur Peterson as Albert Harding. Writer: Bernard Slade. Directed by: Howard Morris.
Samantha, Darrin, and Clara try to help a man who has fallen under a curse put on one of his ancestors by a witch.

No. 40_____

My Grandson, the Warlock 10/7/65
GS: Kendrik Huxham as the warlock, Minnie Coffin as Nanny Witch, Beryl Hammond as the kitty girl.
Writers: Ted Sherdeman and Jane Klove. Directed by: E. W. Swackhamer.
Samantha's father mistakes the Tate's baby for Samantha's, so he tries to teach it to perform witchcraft.

No. 41_____

The Joker Is a Card 10/14/65
GS: Douglas Evans as Mr. Foster. Writer: Ron Friedman.
Directed by: E. W. Swackhamer.
Samantha, Endora and Darrin try to cure Uncle Arthur of his habit of playing practical jokes.

No. 42_____

Take Two Aspirins and Half a Pint of Porpoise Milk 10/21/65
GS: Phillip Coolidge as Trigby, Lauren Gilbert as Norton, Maudie Prickett as the woman on the street, Larry Mann as the police sergeant, Ray Hastings as the first policeman. Writer: Bernard Slade. Directed by: William Asher.
Samantha loses her powers after she is exposed to a black Peruvian rose.

No. 43_____

Trick or Treat 10/28/65
GS: Jack Collins as Jack Rogers, Barbara Drew as Mrs. Rogers, Maureen McCormick as Endora (as a girl), David Bailey as boy magician, Skip Tourgeson as the delivery boy. Writers: Lawrence J. Cohen and Fred Freeman. Directed by: E. W. Swackhamer.
Endora casts a spell on Darrin, which will gradually turn Darrin into a werewolf.

No. 44_____

The Very Informal Dress 11/4/65
GS: Max Showaltzer as Charles Barlow, Hardie Albright as Judge Crosetti, Dick Wilson as Montague, Dick Balduzzi as the first policeman, Gene Darfler as the second policeman. Writers: Paul David and John L. Greene. Directed by: William Asher.
Clara uses her powers to create new clothes for Darrin and Samantha to wear to a dinner engagement. Unfortunately, the clothes disappear while they are still having dinner.

No. 45_____

... And Then I Wrote 11/11/65
GS: Chet Stratton as Capt. Corcoran, Tom Nardini as the Indian, Clan Soule as Dr. Passmore, Eileen O'Neill as Violet, Joanie Larson as the nurse, Bill Dungan as the first vaudeville performer, Skeets Minton as the second vaudeville performer. Writer: Paul Wayne. Directed by: E.W. Swackhamer.
Samantha brings the characters of her Civil War play to life.

No. 46_____

Junior Executive 11/18/65
GS: Billy Mumy as the young Darrin, Oliver McGowan as Mr. Harding, Helene Winston as the matronly lady, Sharon DeBord as the secretary, John Reilly as the first boy, Rory Stevens as the second boy. Writer: Bernard Slade. Directed by: Howard Morris.
Endora turns Darrin into an eight-year-old boy.

No. 47_____

Aunt Clara's Old Flame 11/25/65
GS: Charles Ruggles as Hedley Partridge. Writer: Bernard Slade. Directed by: E.W. Swackhamer.
Aunt Clara's old warlock boyfriend comes for a visit.

No. 48_____

A Strange Little Visitor 12/2/65
GS: Craig Hundley, as Merle Brocken, Anne Sargent as Margaret Brocken, Tim Herbert as the man in the bar, Dick Balduzzi as the policeman, James Doohan as Walter Brocken. Writers: John L. Greene and Paul Davis. Directed by: E.W. Swackhamer.
Samantha watches a ten-year-old warlock while his parents are out of town.

No. 49 _____

My Boss the Teddy Bear 12/9/65
GS: Lon Bentley as the clerk, Jack Collins as Harper, Henry Hunter as Bertram, Jill Foster as the receptionist, Lael Jackson as Diane. Writer: Bernard Slade. Directed by: William Asher.
Darrin thinks Endora has turned Larry into a Teddy Bear.

    Episode #49
Darrin thinks Endora has turned _____ into a _____.
        A. Gladys Kravitz, Cow
        B. Frank Stephens, Mushroom
        C. Larry Tate, Teddy Bear

Answer: C. Larry Tate, Teddy Bear

No. 50 _____

Speak the Truth 12/16/65
GS: Charles Lane as Ed Hotchkiss, Elizabeth Fraser as Frances Hotchkiss, Diana Chesney as Hagatha, Mort Mills as the policeman, Sharon DeBord as Miss Kimball. Writers: Paul David and John L. Greene. Directed by: William Asher.
Endora gives Darrin a statuette which causes anyone who comes near it to tell the absolute truth.

No. 51 _____

A Vision of Sugar Plums 12/23/65
Samantha recalls the time she took an orphan to see Santa Claus. (This is a re-cut version of the episode of the same name, only with a new opening.)

No. 52 _____

The Magic Cabin 12/30/65
GS: Peter Duryea as Charlie McBain, Beryl Hammond as Alice McBain, Sharon DeBord as the Secretary. Writer: Paul Wayne. Directed by: William Asher.
Samantha uses witchcraft to change Larry's old shack into a beautiful cabin

No. 53 _____

Maid to Order 1/6/66
GS: Alice Ghostley as Naomi, Elvia Allman as Mrs. Luftwaffe, Roxanne Arlen as Barbara Elliot. Writer: Richard Baer. Directed by: Bill Asher.
Samantha hires a bumbling maid to do the housework so she can rest until the baby is born.

No. 54 _____

And Then There Were Three 1/13/66
GS: Eve Arden as Nurse Kelton, Bobby Byles as Fred Potter, Gene Blakely as Dave, Joseph Mell as the manager, Mason Curry as Dr. Anton, Celeste Yarnall as the student nurse. Writer: Bernard Slade. Directed by: Bill Asher.
Darrin believes that Endora has turned his newly born daughter Tabitha into a grownup when he sees Samantha's look-alike cousin Serena.

No. 55 _____

My Baby, the Tycoon 1/20/66
GS: Jack Fletcher as Julius, William Kendis as the stock broker. Writer: Richard Baer. Directed by: Bill Asher.
The Kravitzes give Tabitha a share of stock as a gift; when the stock goes up in value, Darrin believes Tabitha did it with witchcraft.

No. 56 _____

Samantha Meets the Folks 1/27/66
Samantha recalls the time she met Darrin's parents for the first time. (This is a re-cut version with new footage of the previous episode of the same name.)

No. 57 _____

Fastest Gun on Madison Avenue 2/3/66
GS: Herbie Faye as Kovack's manager, Rockne Tarkington as the elevator operator, Sid Cane as the waiter, Herb Vigran

as Sam the bartender, Roger Torrey as Joe Kovack, Dick Wilson as the drunk. Writer: Lee Erwin. Directed by: Bill Asher.
Darrin, with Samantha's help, knocks out a boxer and finds himself the number one contender for the boxing title.

No. 58_____

The Dancing Bear 2/10/66
GS: Arthur Julian as Hockstedder. Writer: James Henderson. Directed by: Bill Asher.
Endora creates a dancing teddy bear for Tabitha which Darrin's father tries to sell to a toy manufacturer.

No. 59_____

Double Tate 2/17/66
GS: Irwin Charone as Turgeon, Jill Foster as the secretary, Kathee Francis as Joyce. Writer: Paul Wayne. Directed by: Bill Asher.
Darrin turns himself into an exact double of Larry when Endora grants him three wishes for his birthday.

No. 60_____

Samantha the Dressmaker 2/24/66
GS: Dick Gautier as Aubert, Harry Holcombe as J.T. Glendon, Barbara Morrison as Doris, Arlen Stuart as Ethel, Jannine Grandel as Brigette. Writer: Lee Erwin. Directed by: Bill Asher.
Samantha helps a French dress designer break into the American market.

No. 61_____

The Horse's Mouth 3/3/66
GS: Patty Regan as Dolly, Robert Sorrells as Gus Walters, Sid Clute as Jack. Writers: Paul David and John L. Greene. Directed by: Bill Asher.
Samantha turns a racehorse into a woman who proceeds to help Darrin's friend win at the races.

No. 62_____

Baby's First Paragraph 3/10/66
GS: Clete Roberts, John Newton as the first reporter,
Don Hammer as the second reporter, Robert De Coy
as the postman. Writer: James Henerson. Directed by:
Bill Asher.
Endora causes trouble when she makes baby Tabitha able to talk.

No. 63_____

The Leprechaun 3/17/66
GS: Henry Jones as Brian O'Brian, Parley Baer as Robinson,
Jeff Kirkpatrick as Officer Fogert. Writers: Paul David and
John L. Greene. Directed by: Bill Asher.
Samantha tries to help a leprechaun recover his lost pot of gold.

No. 64_____

Double Split 3/24/66
GS: Martin Ashe as Kabaker, Julie Gregg as Kabaker's
daughter, Dan Tobin as Ames, Ivan Bonar as the desk
clerk. Writer: Howard Leeds. Directed by: Jerry Davis.
Samantha tries to bring Larry and Darrin back together
after they have a fight.

No. 65_____

Disappearing Samantha 4/7/66
GS: Bernard Fox as Osgood Rightmire, Nina Wayne as
Beverly, Foster Brooks as Robert Andrews. Writers: Paul
David and John L. Greene. Directed by: Bill Asher.
Samantha falls under the spell of an ancient ring owned by a man
who debunks witches.

No. 66_____

Follow That Witch (Part I) 4/14/66
GS: Robert Strauss as Charlie Leach, Virginia Martin as
Charmaine Leach, Mary Grace Canfield as Harriet, Steve Franken as

George Barkley, Jack Collins as Robbins, Judy Pace as Miss Perkins, the secretary. Writer: Bernard Slade. Directed by: Bill Asher.
A private detective threatens to expose Samantha as a witch if she does not make him a rich man.

No. 67 _____

Follow The Witch (Part II) 4/21/66
GS: Same credits as Part I with the addition of Jill Foster as Betty, Renie Riano as Mrs. Granite. Writer: Bernard Slade. Directed by: Bill Asher.
Samantha teaches the detective never to blackmail a witch.

No. 68 _____

A Bum Raps 5/5/66
GS: Cliff Hall as Horace, Herbie Faye as William, Henry Hunter as Uncle Albert, Ann Prentiss as the secretary. Writer: Herman Groves. Directed by: Jerry Davis.
Samantha mistakes a con man for Darrin's eccentric Uncle Albert.

No. 69 _____

Divided He Falls 4/28/66
GS: Frank Maxwell as Sanford Stern, Jerry Catron as Joe, Joy Harmon as Francie, Susan Barrett as the girl. Writer: Paul Wayne. Directed by: R. Robert Rosenbaum.
Endora splits Darrin into two people. Darrin #1 is a hard worker while Darrin #2 is an irresponsible fun lover.

No. 70 _____

Man's Best Friend 5/12/66
GS: Richard Dreyfuss as Rodney, Barbara Morrison as Rodney's mother, Mary Grace Canfield as Harriet. Writer: Bernard Slade. Directed by: Jerry Davis.
A neurotic warlock named Rodney tries to break up Samantha's marriage so she can marry him.

No. 71_____

The Catnapper 5/19/66
GS: Marion Thompson as Toni, Robert Strauss as
Charlie Leach, Virginia Martin as Charmaine Leach.
Writer: Howard Leeds. Directed by: R. Robert Rosenbaum.
Endora turns a beautiful client of Darrin's into a cat, which is stolen
by the private detective (from a previous episode).
He promises to return the cat in return for a million dollars.

No. 72_____

What Every Young Man Should Know 5/26/66
Writers: Paul David and John L. Greene. Directed by:
Jerry Davis.
Endora sends Samantha and Darrin back in time to see
if Darrin would have married Samantha if he knew she was a witch.

No. 73_____

The Girl with the Golden Nose 6/2/66
GS: Oliver McGowan as Waterhouse, Steve Rinaldi as
the bellboy, Gene Blakely as Dave, Alice Backers as
Betty, Owen McGiveney as the butler. Writers: Syd Zelinka
and Paul Wayne. Directed by: R. Robert Rosenbaum.
Darrin is convinced that Samantha used witchcraft to gain
a new account, so Samantha tries to show him that he did it by himself.

No. 74_____

Prodigy 6/9/66
GS: Jack Weston as Louis, Lennie Bremen as the cab
driver. Writers: Fred Freeman and Lawrence J. Cohen.
Directed by: Howard Morris.
Samantha tries to help Gladys's brother regain his confidence and play his
violin at a benefit.

Third Season
September 1966 to May 1967

No. 75 _____

Nobody's Perfect 9/15/66
GS: David Lewis as Mark Robbins, Robert Q. Lewis as Diego Fenman, Lindsay Workman as Dr. Koblin. Writer: Doug Tibbles. Directed by: Bill Asher.
Samantha tries to find a way to tell Darrin that Tabitha is a witch like her.

No. 76 _____

The Moment of Truth 9/22/66
Writers: David V. Robinson and John L. Greene.
Directed by: Bill Asher.
Darrin finally learns that Tabitha is a witch. He now has to keep the Tates from finding out when they come for a visit.

No. 77 _____

Witches and Warlocks Are My Favorite Things 9/29/66
GS: Reta Shaw as Hagatha, Estelle Winwood as Enchantra.
Writers: David V. Robinson and John L. Greene. Directed by: William Asher.
Samantha calls for her father when her mother and aunts want to take Tabitha away with them, so she can attend a witches school.

No. 78 _____

Accidental Twins 10/6/66
Writer: Howard Leeds. Directed by: William Asher.
While baby sitting, Clara accidentally turns the Tate's baby son into twins.

No. 79 _____

A Most Unusual Wood Nymph 10/13/66
GS: Michael Ansara as Rufus the Red, Henry Corden as Muldoon, Kathleen Nolan as Gerry O'Toole, Jean

Blake as the maid. Writer: Ed Jurist. Directed by: Bill Asher.
A wood nymph reveals to Samantha that she has been sent to plague Darrin because his ancestor slew her master, Refus The Red. So Samantha goes back in time to prevent Darrin The Bold from killing Rufus.

No. 80 _____

Endora Moves In for a Spell 10/20/66
GS: Paul Smith as Floyd, Sid Clute as Noel, Arthur Adams as the desk sergeant. Writer: Robert Riley Crutcher. Directed by: William Asher.
Endora and Uncle Arthur have a fight, claiming each is a bad influence on Tabitha.

No. 81 _____

Twitch or Treat 10/27/66
GS: Barry Atwater as Boris, Joan Huntington as Eva, Willie Mays as himself, Jim Begg as Morgan. Writers: Robert Riley Crutcher and James Henerson. Directed by: Bill Asher.
Endora holds a wild Halloween party in their house. Uncle Arthur and Samantha try to get rid or her and the party.

No. 82 _____

Dangerous Diaper Dan 11/3/66
GS: Marty Ingels as Dan, Dawn Keefer as Kimberley, Alex Gerry as Mr. Wright, Jim Begg as Peterson, Bill Beck as the bartender. Writers: David Braverman and Bob Marcus. Directed by: William Asher.
A diaper serviceman gives Tabitha a rattle with a microphone in it. He is actually a spy for another advertising agency and wants to listen in on Darrin's conversation so he can steal his ideas.

"Dangerous Diaper Dan" Quotes:
Samantha: "I have a good mind to go home to mother."
Darrin: "What for? Your mother is always here!"

No. 83_____

The Short Happy Circuit of Aunt Clara 11/10/66
GS: Reginald Owen as Ocky, Arte Julian as MacElroy,
Leo DeLyon as Jenkins. Writer: Lee Erwin. Directed by:
Bill Asher.
Aunt Clara, who is depressed because her warlock boyfriend
left her for a younger woman, thinks she caused a power
blackout all over town.

No. 84_____

I'd Rather Twitch Than Fight 11/17/66
GS: Bridget Hanley as the salesgirl, James Millhollin
as the salesman, Norman Fell as Dr. Freud, Burt Mustin
as the old man, Parley Baer as Dr. Kramer, Riza Royce as
the salesgirl. Writer: James Henerson. Directed by: R. Robert
Rosenbaum.
Endora summons Sigmund Freud to help Samantha and
Darrin's marriage problems.

"I'd Rather Twitch Than Fight" Quotes:
Louise: "What did that hounds tooth sports jacket represent to Darrin?"
Samantha: "Bad taste?"

No. 85_____

Oedipus Hex 11/24/66
GS: Ned Glass as the milkman, Irwin Charone as the
Parkinson, Paul Smith as the policeman, Paul Dooley as the
TV man. Writers: David V. Robinson and John L. Greene.
Directed by: Bill Asher.
Endora creates some magic popcorn, which will cause anyone
who eats it to become lazy and refuse to work.

No. 86_____

Sam's Spooky Chair 12/1/66
GS: J. Pat O'Malley as Max Cosgrove, Roger Garrett
as Clyde, Anne Seymour as Adelaide Cosgrove, Howard

Morton as the salesman. Writer: Coslough Johnson. Directed by: R. Robert Rosenbaum.
Samantha finds that the antique chair she bought is actually her old warlock boyfriend, whom she rejected years earlier.

No. 87_____

My Friend Ben (Part I) 12/8/66
GS: Fredd Wayne as Ben Franklin, Mike Road as Hawkins, Tim Rooney as the teenager, Billy Beck as as the first man, Harry Holcomb as the judge, Donald Mitchell as the policeman. Writer: James Henerson. Directed by: Bill Asher.
Aunt Clara accidentally summons Benjamin Franklin to help Samantha fix her lamp.

No. 88_____

Samantha for the Defense (Part II) 12/15/66
GS: Same as Part I with the addition of Jonathan Hole as the principal, Paul Sand as Whalen, Violet Carlson as the librarian, Tim Rooney, Billy Beck, Martin Ashe as Pierce, Don Steele as himself. Writer: James Henderson. Directed by: William Asher.
Samantha defends Benjamin Franklin at his trial when he is accused of stealing a fire engine.

"Samantha for the Defense" Quotes:
Darrin to Benjamin Franklin: "Didn't you once say, 'Early to bed, early to rise, makes a man healthy, wealthy, and wise'?"
Benjamin Franklin: "Yes, I did, but that was before the electric light."

No. 89_____

A Gazebo Never Forgets 12/22/66
GS: Paul Reed as Mr. Scranton, Steve Franken as Hawkins. Writers: Jerry Devine and Izzy Elinson. Directed by: R. Robert Rosenbaum.
Clara accidentally creates a live baby elephant in the middle of the living room and can't remember how to get rid of it.

No. 90_____

Soapbox Derby 12/29/66
GS: Michael Shea as Johnny, William Bramley as
Mills, Peter Dunhill as flash, George Andre as the
announcer. Writer: James Henerson. Directed by:
Alan Jay Factor.
Samantha helps a boy win a race and his father's approval at the same time.

No. 91_____

Sam in the Moon 1/5/67
GS: Dort Clark as Ed, Tim Herbert as Frank, Joseph Mell
as Grand, Baynes Barron as Harry, Bob Okazaki as Mr.
Watanabe. Writer: James Henerson. Directed by: R. Robert
Rosenbaum.
Darrin dreams what might happen if he told NASA authorities
about Samantha and her frequent visits to the moon.

No. 92_____

Hoho the Clown 1/12/67
GS: Joey Foreman as HoHo, Dick Wilson as Mr. Solow,
Charles J. Stewart as the producer. Writer: Richard Baer.
Directed by: William Asher.
Endora casts a spell on a TV clown to perform his show only for Tabitha.

No. 93_____

Super Car 1/19/67
GS: Dave Madden as Joe, Irwin Charone as Sheldrake,
Herb Ellis as Charlie. Writer: Ed Jurist. Directed by:
William Asher.
Endora gives Darrin the prototype of a new car, which she stole
from its creator, one of Darrin's clients.

No. 94_____

The Corn Is as High as a Guernsey's Eye 1/26/67
GS: Don Penny as Barney, Howard Smith as C. L.

Morton, Joseph Perry as Mr. Henderson, Art Lewis
as Mr. Culpepper, William Thegoe as Mr. Whittle.
Writer: Ruth Brooks Flippen. Directed by: Bill Asher.
Samantha thinks Clara turned herself accidentally into a cow and takes it home with her.

No. 95 _____

Trial and Error of Aunt Clara 2/2/67
GS: Arthur Malet as the judge, Nancy Andrews as Hagatha,
Ottola Nesmith as Enchantra. Writer: Ed Jurist. Directed by:
William Asher.
Samantha defends Clara when the Witches council wants to banish
her because of her failing powers.

No. 96 _____

Three Wishes 2/9/67
GS: Linda Gaye Scott as Buffy, Edythe Sills as the secretary,
Robert Stiles as the Western Union boy. Writer: Robert
Riley Crutcher. Directed by: Bill Asher.
Endora gives Darrin three wishes, in order to trap him with another woman.

No. 97 _____

I Remember You.... Sometimes 2/16/67
GS: Dan Tobin as Ed Pennybaker, Grace Albertson as
Cynthia Pennybaker, Jill Foster as the secretary. Writers:
David V. Robinson and John L. Greene. Directed by: Bill
Asher.
Endora casts a spell on Darrin's watch, so that whenever he wears it he
will have a perfect memory.

No. 98 _____

Art for Sam's Sake 2/23/67
GS: Arthur Julian as Cunningham, Tom Palmer as the
chairman, Mickey Deems as Jenkins, Paul Sorensen as
O'Leary, John Alonzo as the guard. Writer: Jack Sher.

Directed by: Bill Asher.
Endora switches a masterpiece for Samantha's painting at a charity exhibit.

No. 99_____

Charlie Harper, Winner 3/2/67
GS: Angus Duncan as Charlie Harper, Joanna Moore as Daphne Harper, Henry Hunter as Sen. Ross, Karl Redcoff as Count Darvi, Teresa Tudor as the Countessa. Writer: Earl Barrett. Directed by: R. Robert Rosenbaum.
Darrin and Samantha try to compete with Darrin's old college rival who is a bragging millionaire.

No. 100_____

Aunt Clara's Victoria Victory 3/9/67
GS: Jane Connell as Queen Victoria, Robert H. Harris as Morgan. Writer: Robert Riley Crutcher. Directed by: William Asher.
Aunt Clara accidentally summons Queen Victoria to the Stephen's house.

Trivia Tidbit:
Aunt Clara mentions that she was once a lady-in-waiting to Queen Victoria.

No. 101_____

The Crone of Cawdor 3/16/67
GS: Julie Gregg as Terry Warbell, Dorothy Neumann as the Crone of Cawdor, Robert P. Lieb as Jay Warbell, Heather Woodruff as the secretary, Del Press as Miss Kornblut. Writer: Ed Jurist. Directed by: R. Robert Rosenbaum.
Samantha has to prevent Darrin from kissing a young girl, actually the Crone of Cawdor who has taken over the body of the girl. If he kisses her, he will age 500 years.

Trivia Tidbit:
In this episode, Samantha and Darrin try to celebrate the anniversary of their first meeting by going to La Bella Donna for lunch, however, Larry ruins it for them.

No. 102_____

No More, Mr. Nice Guy 3/23/67
GS: Larry D. Mann as Baldwin, George Ives as Farnsworth,
Judson Pratt as Eastwood, Judy Lang as Gloria, Dick Wilson
as Harry, Paul Barselow as Max, Heather Woodruff.
Writer: Jack Sher. Directed by: Bill Asher.
Endora casts a spell on Darrin, which makes everyone hate him.

Trivia Tidbit:
Darrin says he voted for Mayor Rocklin.
George Ives played Captain Kelly in Episode #18, "The Cat's Meow", and as client O.J. Slocum in Episode #139, "Man of the Year."
No. 103_____

It's Wishcraft 3/30/67
Writer: James Henerson. Directed by: Paul Davis.
Darrin is afraid that his visiting parents will learn that Tabitha is a witch.

"It's Wishcraft" Quotes:
Phyllis Stephens: "I get such a terrible head cold whenever I fly."
Endora: "Oh, really? I never do."

Phyllis Stephens: "His name is Dobbin! I mean Darrin."

Phyllis Stephens approaching Endora: "Do you live here now?"

Trivia Tidbit:
Mrs. Phyllis Stephens actually kisses Samantha hello in Episode #103, "It's Wishcraft".

No. 104_____

How to Fail in Business with All Kinds of Help 4/6/67
GS: Henry Beckman as Mr. Wilkerson, Lisa Kirk as
Mme. Marushka, Jill Foster as the secretary, Myra de Groot
as the receptionist, Ralph Brooks as the bartender. Writer:
Ron Friedman. Directed by: Richard Kinon.
Darrin thinks a domineering businesswoman is really Endora in disguise.

Trivia Tidbit:
Endora gives her "Born in the sparkle of the star" speech
"We are quicksilver, a fleeting shadow, a distant sound. Our home has no boundaries beyond which we cannot pass. We live in music, in a flash of color. We live on the wind and
In the Sparkle of a star."-Endora (originally heard in Episode #2, "Be It Ever So Mortgaged.")

No. 105 _____

***Bewitched*, Bothered and Infuriated** 4/13/67
GS: George Lymburn as the man, Jack Fletcher as the manager. Writer: Howard Leeds. Directed by: R. Robert Rosenbaum.
Samantha tries to prevent Larry from breaking his leg on his second honeymoon.

No. 106 _____

Nobody But a Frog Knows How to Live 4/27/67
GS: John Fiedler as Fergus F. Finglehoff, Dan Tobin as Saunders, Corin Camcho as Phoebe. Writer: Ruth Brooks Flippen. Directed by: Richard Kinon.
Samantha tries to help a frog, who was transformed into a man, change back into a frog again.

No. 107 _____

There's Gold in Them Thar Pills 5/4/67
GS: Milton Frome as Hornbeck, Allen Davis as the lawyer, Mark Harris as the tailor, Stuart Nesbit as the boat salesman, Pat McCaffrie as the realtor. Writers: Paul Wayne and Ed Jurist. Directed by: R. Robert Rosenbaum.
Darrin and Larry plan to sell Dr. Bombay's cold pills on the open market, unaware that he is a warlock who treats only witches.

Fourth Season
September 1967 to May 1968

No. 108_____

Long Live the Queen 9/7/67
GS: Ruth McDevitt. Writer: Ed Jurist. Director: William Asher
The queen of the witches decides to abdicate in favor of Samantha.

No. 109_____

Toys in Babeland 9/14/67
GS: Paul Barselow. Writer: Ed Jurist. Director: William Asher
Tabitha brings all of her toys to life.

No. 110_____

Business, Italian Style 9/21/67
GS: Renzo Cesana. Writer: Michael Morris. Director: William Asher.
Endora casts a spell on Darrin, which causes him to speak only Italian.

No. 111_____

Double, Double, Toil and Trouble 9/28/67
GS: Stanley Beck. Writer: Ed Jurist. Director: William Asher
Endora summons Serena to take Samantha's place in order to break up her marriage.

No. 112_____

Cheap, Cheap! 10/5/67
GS: Parley Baer. Writer: Ed Jurist. Director: William Asher
Endora casts a spell, which turns Darrin into a miser.

No. 113_____

No Zip in My Zap 10/12/67
GS: Mala Powers. Writer: Barbara Avedon. Director: Richard Kinon.
Darrin's old girlfriend comes for a visit, jus as Samantha loses her powers.

No. 114_____

Birdies, Bogies and Baxter 10/19/67
GS: MacDonald Carey. Writers: John L. Greene and David V. Robinson. Director: William Asher.
Endora puts a spell on Darrin's golf clubs, which will make him make fantastic shots no matter how badly he plays.

No. 115_____

The Safe and Sane Halloween 10/26/67
GS: Jerry Maren, Felix Silla, Billy Curtis. Writer: James Henerson. Director: William Asher
Tabitha causes the characters in a Halloween picture book to come to life.

No. 116_____

Out of Sync, Out of Mind 11/2/67
Writer: Ed Jurist. Director: Richard Kinon.
Aunt Clara accidentally casts a spell, which causes Samantha to speak out of sync. She moves her lips and then her voice is heard later.

No. 117_____

That Was No Chick, That Was My Wife 11/9/67
GS: Herb Voland, Sara Seegar. Writer: Rick Mittleman. Director: William Asher.
Darrin almost loses his job when Samantha appears in New York and Chicago at the same time.

No. 118 _____

Allergic to Macedonian Dodo Birds 11/16/67
GS: Janos Prohaska. Writer: Richard Baer. Director: Richard Kinon.
Endora's powers are transferred to Clara, when she comes in   contact with a Dodo bird.

No. 119 _____

Samantha's Thanksgiving to Remember 11/23/67
GS: Jacques Aubuchon, Richard Bull, Laurie Main. Writer:
Tom and Helen August. Director: Richard Kinon.
Aunt Clara accidentally transfers herself, the Stephens's and Mrs. Kravitz to 17th-century Plymouth on Thanksgiving Day, where Darrin finds himself accused of witchcraft.

No. 120 _____

Solid Gold Mother-in-Law 11/30/67
GS: Jack Collins. Writer: Robert Crutcher. Director: R. Robert Rosenbaum.
Endora turns Darrin into a pony and Samantha persuades her mother to change him back.

No. 121 _____

My What Big Ears You Have 12/7/67
GS: Joan Hotchkiss, Myra de Groot, and Tom Browne. Writer:
Ed Jurist. Director: Richard Kinon.
Endora casts a spell on Darrin, which will cause his ears to grow every time he tells a lie.

No. 122 _____

I Get Your Nanny, You Get My Goat 12/14/67
GS: Reginald Gardiner, Hermione Baddeley. Writer: Ron Friedman. Director: William Asher.
An old warlock puts a spell on Darrin, when he believes Darrin has stolen his servant.

No. 123_____

Humbug Not to Be Spoken Here 12/21/67
GS: Charles Lane, Don Beddoe. Writers: Lila Garrett, Bernie Kahn. Director: William Asher.
Samantha tries to teach a lonely old man the meaning of Christmas.

No. 124_____

Samantha's Da Vinci Dilemma 12/28/67
GS: John Abbott. Writers: Jerry Mayer, Paul L. Friedman. Director: Richard Kinon.
Aunt Clara summons Da Vinci to paint Samantha's house.

No. 125_____

Once in a Vial 1/4/68
GS: Henry Beckman, Ron Randell, Arch Johnson. Writers: James Henerson, Ed Jurist. Director: Bruce Bilson.
Endora drinks a love potion she had intended for Samantha, causing her to fall for one of Darrin's clients.

No. 126_____

Snob in the Grass (Part I) 1/11/68
GS: Nancy Kovack, Frank Wilcox. Writer: Ed Jurist. Director: R. Robert Rosenbaum.
Darrin's old girlfriend tries to show off and upstage Samantha.

No. 127_____

If They Never Met (Part II) 1/25/68
GS: Nancy Kovack. Writers: Bill Idelson, Samuel Bobrick. Director: R. Robert Rosenbaum.
Endora returns Darrin to a time before he met Samantha to see if he would be happy without her.

No. 128_____

Hippie, Hippie, Hippie 2/1/68
GS: Ralph Story. Writer: Michael Morris. Director: William Asher.
When Serena is arrested at a hippie love-in and gets her picture in the papers, everyone thinks it is Samantha.

No. 129_____

A Prince for a Day 2/8/68
GS: William Bassett, Stuart Margolin. Writer: Ed Jurist.
Director: R. Robert Rosenbaum.
Tabitha summons Prince Charming out of her Sleeping Beauty storybook, but can't send him back.

No. 130_____

McTavish 2/15/68
GS: Ronald Long, Reginald Owen. Writer: James Henerson.
Director: Paul Davis.
Samantha convinces a ghost to stop haunting a castle, but regrets her action when he decides to haunt the Stephens's house instead.

No. 131_____

How Green Was My Grass 2/29/68
GS: Richard X. Slattery. Writer: Ed Jurist. Director: R. Robert Rosenbaum.
A synthetic lawn is accidentally installed at the Stephens's house which causes Darrin to think Samantha created the new lawn with her powers.

No. 132_____

To Twitch or Not to Twitch 3/14/68
GS: Jean Blake, Margaret Muse. Writers: Lila Garrett, Bernie Kahn. Director: William Asher.
Darrin and Samantha have a fight when he demands that she should not use her powers.

No. 133_____

Playmates 3/21/68
GS: Peggy Pope. Writer: Richard Baer. Director: William Asher.
Tabitha turns a little bully into a bulldog.

No. 134_____

Tabitha's Cranky Spell 3/28/68
GS: J. Edward McKinley, Sara Seegar. Writer: Robert Riley.
Director: William Asher.
A ghost asks Samantha to help him stop his nephew
from ruining his company.

No. 135_____

I Confess 4/4/68
GS: Woodrow Parfrey. Writer: Richard Baer. Director:
Seymour Robbie.
Samantha shows Darrin what would happen to their life together if
she were to tell everyone that she is a witch.

No. 136_____

A Majority of Two 4/11/68
GS: Richard Hayden, Helen Funai. Writer: Ed Jurist. Director:
R. Robert Rosenbaum.
Samantha entertains a Japanese client who falls for Aunt Clara.

No. 137_____

Samantha's Secret Saucer 4/18/68
GS: Hamilton Camp, Steve Franken. Writers: Jerry Mayer,
Paul L. Friedman. Director: Richard Michaels.
Aunt Clara accidentally transports a spaceship with two dog like
aliens into Samantha's backyard.

No. 138_____

The No-Harm Charm 4/25/68
GS: Vaughn Taylor. Writer: Ed Jurist. Director: Russell B. Mayberry.
Uncle Arthur plays a joke on Darrin when he gives him a charm which will protect him from witchcraft and other disasters.

No. 139_____

Man of the Year 5/2/68
GS: Roland Winters. Writer: John L. Greene. Director: R. Robert Rosenbaum.
Endora casts a magic circle around Darrin. Anyone who comes within the circle will be charmed by him.

No. 140_____

Splitsville 5/16/68
GS: Arthur Julian. Writer: Richard Baer. Director: William Asher.
Gladys has a fight with Abner and moves in with Samantha and Darrin.

No. 141_____

Samantha's Wedding Present 9/26/68
GS: Dick Wilson, Jack Griffin. Writer: Bernard Slade. Director: William Asher.
Endora Casts a spell, which causes Darrin to gradually shrink in size.

No. 142_____

Samantha Goes South for a Spell 10/3/68
GS: Isabel Sanford, Jack Cassidy. Writer: Ed Jurist. Director: William Asher.
A jealous witch mistakes Samantha for Serena and sends her back to Old New Orleans in 1868.

No. 143_____

Samantha on the Keyboard 10/10/68
GS: Jonathan Harris, Fritz Feld. Writer: Richard Baer. Director: Richard Michaels.
Endora uses witchcraft to turn Tabitha into a magnificent piano player.

No. 144_____

Darrin Gone! And Forgotten? 10/17/68
GS: Steve Franken, Mercedes McCambridge. Writers: Lila Garrett, Bernie Kahn. Director: William Asher.
A mean witch threatens to destroy Darrin unless Samantha consents to marry her overprotected son.

No. 145_____

It's So Nice to Have a Spouse Around the House
10/24/68
GS: Fifi D'Orsay. Writer: Barbara Avedon. Director: William Asher.
Darrin takes Samantha on a second honeymoon unaware that he has really taken Serena, not Samantha, on their trip.

No. 146_____

Mirror, Mirror on the Wall 11/7/68
GS: Herb Voland. Writers: Lila Garrett, Bernie Kahn. Director: Richard Michaels.
Endora turns Darrin into the most self-centered and vain man in the world.

No. 147_____

Samantha's French Pastry 11/14/68
GS: Henry Gibson. Writer: Richard Baer. Director: William Asher.
Uncle Arthur accidentally conjures up Napoleon and finds he can't remember how to send them back.

No. 148_____

Is It Magic or Imagination 11/21/68
GS: Dick Wilson. Writer: Arthur Julian. Director: Luther James.
Darrin thinks Samantha won a slogan contest by using witchcraft.

No. 149_____

Samantha Fights City Hall 11/28/68
GS: Arch Johnson, Vic Tayback. Writer: Rick Mittleman.
Director: Richard Michaels.
Samantha fights to keep a new supermarket from taking the place of a neighborhood park.

No. 150_____

Samantha Loses Her Voice 12/5/68
Writers: Lila Garrett, Bernie Kahn. Director: William Asher.
Uncle Arthur plays another practical joke when he switches Darrin's and Samantha's voices.

No. 151_____

I Don't Want to Be a Toad 12/12/68
GS: Maudie Prickett, Art Metrano, Paul Sorenson.
Writer: Doug Tibbles. Director: Richard Michaels.
Tabitha changes a classmate named Amy into a butterfly.

No. 152_____

Weep No More, My Willow 12/19/68
GS: Paul Sorenson, Jean Blake. Writer: Michael Morris.
Director: William Asher.
Dr. Bombay's spell to save a weeping willow tree backfires when it causes Samantha to weep uncontrollably.

No. 153 _____

Instant Courtesy 12/26/68
GS: Mala Powers. Writer: Arthur Alsberg. Director: R. Robert Rosenbaum.
Endora turns Darrin into a perfect gentleman, in order to teach him a lesson for being rude to her.

No. 154 _____

Samantha's Super Maid 1/2/69
GS: Virginia Gregg, Nellie Burt. Writers: Peggy Chantler Dick, Douglas Dick. Director: R. Robert Rosenbaum.
Samantha hires a maid who is so devoted to her job that nothing anyone does can get her to leave.

No. 155 _____

Cousin Serena Strikes Again (Part I) 1/9/69
GS: Nancy Kovack. Writer: Ed Jurist. Director: Richard Michaels.
Serena turns Darrin's client into a monkey, when she made a play for Darrin behind Samantha's back.

No. 156 _____

Cousin Serena Strikes Again (Part II) 1/16/69
GS: Nancy Kovack, Cliff Norton, Richard X. Slattery. Writer: Ed Jurist. Director: Richard Michaels.
Samantha has to try to capture the client turned monkey after it escapes from the house, so Serena can change her back.

No. 157

One Touch of Midas 1/23/69
GS: Cliff Norton, Meg Wyllie. Writers: Jerry Mayer, Paul L. Friedman. Director: Richard Michaels.
Darrin falls under the spell of a magical doll called The Fuzz, and anyone who touches it becomes overly generous.

No. 158_____

Samantha the Bard 1/30/69
GS: Larry D. Mann. Writer: Richard Baer. Director: Richard Michaels.
Endora goes to find Dr. Bombay in order to help Samantha, who finds that everything she says comes out in rhyme.

No. 159_____

Samantha the Sculptress 2/6/69
GS: Cliff Norton. Writer: Doug Tibbles. Director: William Asher.
Endora causes trouble when she brings Samantha's bust of Darrin to life.

No. 160_____

Mrs. Stephens, Where Are You? 2/13/69
GS: Hal England, Ruth McDevitt. Writers: Peggy Chantler Dick, Douglas Dick. Director: Richard Michaels.
Serena turns Darrin's mother into a cat.

No. 161_____

Marriage, Witch's Style 2/20/69
GS: John Fiedler, Lloyd Bochner, Peter Brocco. Writer: Michael Morris. Director: William Asher.
Serena decides she wants to marry a mortal and settle down like Samantha.

No. 162_____

Going Ape 2/27/69
GS: Lou Antonio. Writers: Lila Garrett, Bernie Kahn. Director: Richard Michaels.
Samantha turns a chimp into a man for a day.

No. 163_____

Tabitha's Weekend 3/6/69
Writers: Peggy Chantler Dick, Douglas Dick. Director:
R. Robert Rosenbaum.
When Endora and Darrin's mother have a fight,
Tabitha, believing she is the cause, turns herself
into a cookie.

No. 164_____

The Battle of Burning Oak 3/13/69
GS: Edward Andrews, Harriet MacGibbon. Writers: Pauline &
Leo Townsend. Director: R. Robert Rosenbaum.
Endora turns Darrin into a snob when he joins a country
club.

No. 165_____

Samantha's Power Failure 3/20/69
GS: Ron Masak. Writers: Lila Garrett, Bernie Kahn. Director:
William Asher.
Samantha loses her powers when she refuses to obey the witches council
and give up Darrin. Arthur and Serena also lose their powers because
they sided with her, so they get regular jobs in a candy factory.

No. 166_____

Twitching for UNICEF 3/27/69
GS: Bernie Kopell. Writer: Ed Jurist. Director: William Asher.
Samantha uses witchcraft to make a millionaire make good his $10,000 pledge
to UNICEF.

No. 167_____

Daddy Does His Thing 4/3/69
GS: Mercedes Moliner, Karl Lukas, Shiva Rozier. Writer: Michael Morris. Director: William Asher.
Maurice turns Darrin into a mule when he refuses the magical lighter he gave him for his birthday.

No. 168_____

Samantha's Good News 4/10/69
GS: Murray Matheson. Writer: Richard Baer. Director: Richard Michaels.
Endora and Maurice have a fight when he starts dating a young secretary. Samantha stops their fighting when she announces that she is going to have another baby.

No. 169_____

Samantha's Shopping Spree 4/17/69
GS: Steve Franken, Dave Madden. Writer: Richard Baer. Director: Richard Michaels.
Samantha's cousin Henry, a prankster, causes havoc when he goes shopping with Samantha and Tabitha.

No. 170_____

Samantha and Darrin in Mexico City 4/24/69
GS: Thomas Gomez. Writer: John L. Greene. Director: R. Robert Rosenbaum.
While in Mexico, Endora casts a spell on Darrin, which causes him to disappear whenever he speaks in Spanish. * Dick York's last appearance on *Bewitched*.

No. 171

Sam and the Beanstock 9/18/69
GS: Ronald Long, Johnnie Whitaker, Bobo Lewis.
Writer: Michael Morris. Director: Richard Michaels.
Tabitha brings her storybook of Jack and the
Beanstalk to life and changes places with Jack
when she thinks her parents like boys better
than girls. *Dick Sargent's first appearance as
Darrin Stephens.

No. 172

Samantha's Yoo Hoo Maid 9/25/69
GS: J. Edward McKinley. Writer: Ed Jurist. Director: William Asher.
Endora brings a bumbling witch to act as Samantha's new maid.

118   The Magic of Bewitched Trivia

No. 173_____

Samantha's Caesar Salad 10/2/69
GS: Jay Robinson. Writer: Ed Jurist. Director: William Asher.
Esmeralda tries to create a Caesar salad, but conjures up Julius Caesar instead.

No. 174_____

Samantha's Curious Cravings 10/9/69
GS: William Schallert. Writers: Fred Freeman, Lawrence J. Cohen. Director: Richard Michaels.
Samantha finds that whatever she craves comes to her magically.

No. 175_____

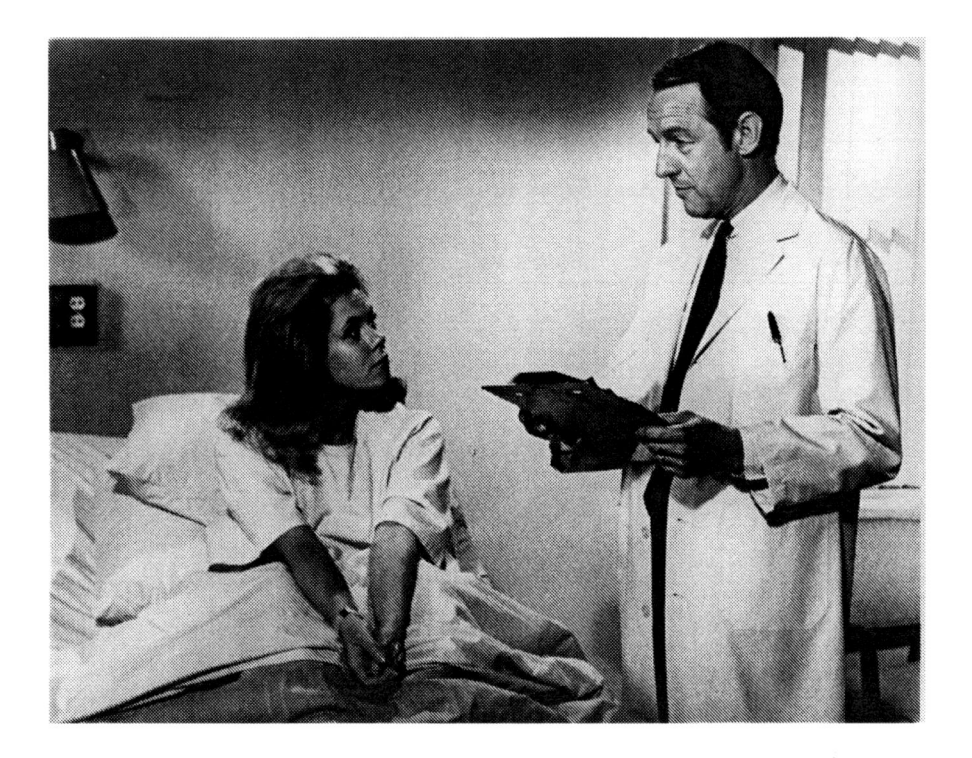

And Something Makes Four 10/16/69
GS: Art Metrano, Pat Priest. Writer: Richard Baer. Director: Richard Michaels.
Maurice casts a spell over his new grandson, that whoever looks at him immediately likes him.

No. 176_____

Naming Samantha's New Baby 10/23/69
Writer: Ed Jurist. Director: William Asher.
Maurice puts Darrin inside a mirror when he finds out that the new baby will be named after Darrin's father and not him.

No. 177

To Trick-or-Treat or Not to Trick-or-Treat 10/30/69
GS: Larry D. Mann, Paul Sorensen, Judy March, Jeanne Sorel.
Writer: Shirley Gordon. Director: William Asher.
Darrin and Endora have a fight over the value
of Halloween.

No. 178_____

A Bunny for Tabitha 11/6/69
GS: Bernie Kopell, Carol Wayne. Writer: Ed Jurist. Director: William Asher.
Uncle Arthur performs a magic act for Tabitha's birthday party. He accidentally conjures up a playboy bunny instead of a bunny rabbit, and can't send her back.

No. 179_____

Samantha's Secret Spell 11/13/69
GS: Bernie Kopell. Writer: Ed Jurist. Director: Richard Michaels.
Samantha tries to prevent Endora's spell to turn Darrin into a mouse at midnight from taking effect.

No. 180_____

Daddy Comes to Visit (Part I) 11/20/69
GS: John Fiedler. Writer: Rick Mittleman. Director: Richard Michaels.
On his birthday, Maurice gives Darrin a watch, which will give him magic powers.

No. 181_____

Darrin the Warlock (Part II) 11/27/69
GS: John Fiedler, J. Edward McKinley, Irene Byatt. Writer: Rick Mittleman. Director: Richard Michaels.
Darrin becomes obsessed with his new powers and refuses to give them up.

No. 182

Sam's Double Mother Trouble 12/4/69
GS: Jane Connell. Writer: Peggy Chantler Dick, Douglas Dick.
Director: David White.
Esmeralda, while reading to Tabitha, accidentally conjures up Mother Goose
just as Darrin's mother comes for a visit.

No. 183

You're So Agreeable 12/11/69
GS: Charles Lane. Writer: Ed Jurist. Director: Luther James.
Endora casts a spell that makes Darrin agree with everyone and everything.

No. 184 _____

Santa Comes to Visit and Stays and Stays 12/18/69
GS: Ronald Long. Writer: Ed Jurist. Director: Richard Michaels.
Esmeralda conjures up Santa Claus.

No. 185 _____

Samantha's Better Halves 1/1/70
GS: Richard Loo. Writers: Lila Garrett, Bernie Kahn.
Director: William Asher.
Endora splits Darrin in two so he can stay home with Samantha as well as go
to Japan to entertain a client.

No. 186 _____

Samantha's Lost Weekend 1/8/70
GS: Bernie Kopell, Pat Priest, Jonathan Hole, Merie Earle.
Writer: Richard Baer. Director: Richard Michaels.
Samantha drinks a glass of milk, on which Esmeralda cast
a spell, which causes her to have an insatiable appetite.

No. 187 _____

The Phrase Is Familiar 1/15/70
GS: Jay Robinson, Cliff Norton, Todd Baron. Writer: Jerry Mayer.
Director: Richard Michaels.
Endora causes Darrin to speak in clichés whenever he opens
his mouth. At the same time, Tabitha's tutor conjures
up the Artful Dodger out of Oliver Twist.

No. 188_____

Samantha's Secret Is Discovered 1/22/70
GS: Bernie Kopell. Writers: Lila Garrett and Bernie Kahn.
Director: William Asher.
Samantha tells Darrin's mother that she is a witch. Thinking she has lost her mind, she goes to a sanitarium where Samantha switches her tranquilizers to hallucinogenic. This way her mother-in-law will think everything that happened was caused by taking the wrong pill. *This episode is not run by many stations, due to the episode's
drug-related story.

No. 189_____

Tabitha's Very Own Samantha 1/29/70
GS: Sara Seegar, Parley Baer. Writer: Shirley Gordon. Director: William Asher.
Tabitha creates a duplicate Samantha to play with her when the real Samantha has to take care of her little brother Adam.

No. 190_____

Super Arthur 2/5/70
GS: Paul Smith, Bernie Kuby. Writer: Ed Jurist. Director: Richard Michaels.
When Arthur takes a pill given to him by Doctor Bombay, it causes him to become everything he thinks about, including Superman.

No. 191_____

What Makes Darrin Run? 2/12/70
GS: Leon Ames. Writers: Lila Garett and Bernie Kahn. Director: William Asher.
Endora casts a spell on Darrin, which makes him more ambitious.

No. 192_____

Serena Stops the Show 2/19/70
GS: Tommy Boyce & Bobby Hart, Art Metrano. Writer: Richard Baer.
Director: Richard Michaels.
Serena tries to get the singing team of Boyce and Hart to sing at the Cosmos Cotillion, an annual dinner dance for witches and warlocks.

No. 193_____

Just a Kid Again 2/26/70
GS: Richard Powell, Ron Masak. Writer: Jerry Mayer.
Director: Richard Michaels.
Tabitha turns a toy salesman into a nine-year-old boy.

No. 194_____

The Generation Zap 3/5/70
GS: Melodie Johnson, Arch Johnson. Writer: Ed Jurist
Director: William Asher.
Serena turns a daughter of a client into a hippie.

No. 195_____

Okay, Who's the Wise Witch 3/12/70
Writer: Richard Baer. Director: Richard Michaels.
A vapor lock caused by Samantha's non-use of
her witchcraft seals the house so no one can
get in or out.

No. 196_____

A Chance on Love 3/19/70
GS: Jack Cassidy. Writer: John L. Greene. Director:
Richard Michaels.
A playboy client mistakes Samantha for Serena.

No. 197_____

If the Shoe Pinches 3/26/70
GS: Henry Gibson. Writer: Ed Jurist. Director: William Asher.
The witches council sends a leprechaun to find the breaking point
of the Stephens's marriage.

No. 198_____

Mona Sammy 4/2/70
Writer: Michael Morris. Director: William Asher.
Larry and Louise mistake a Mona Lisa type painting as being of
Samantha and the artist as being Darrin. In order of Darrin to
keep his job he must paint a portrait of Louise. Samantha
casts a spell on Darrin that will make him a great painter.

No. 199_____

Turn on the Old Charm 4/9/70
GS: John Fiedler. Writer: Richard Baer. Director: Richard Michaels.
Samantha gives Darrin an amulet that causes Endora to be nice to Darrin.

No. 200_____

Make Love Not Hate 4/16/70
GS: Charles Lane, Sara Seegar, Cliff Norton.
Writer: Ed Jurist. Director: William Asher.
Samantha accidentally pours a love potion into the clam dip she plans to serve to Darrin's client. It causes everyone who eats it to fall in love with the first person they see.

No. 201_____

To Go or Not to Go, That is the Question 9/24/70
GS: Jane Connell. Writer: Michael Morris. Director: William Asher.
The High Priestess of Witchdom comes to view Samantha and Darrin's marriage, to decide whether or not she should dissolve the marriage.

No. 202_____

Salem, Here We Come 10/1/70
GS: Jane Connell. Writer: Michael Morris. Director: William Asher.
Samantha arranges that the decision to end their marriage be delayed by fixing up Hepzibah with one of Darrin's clients.

No. 203_____

The Salem Saga 10/8/70
GS: Joan Hotchkis, Dick Wilson. Writer: Ed Jurist. Director: William Asher.
Samantha and Darrin are followed by a bed warmer which came from the House of The Seven Gables.

No. 204_____

Samantha's Hot Bed warmer 10/15/70
GS: Noam Pitlik, Joan Hotchkis. Writer: Ed Jurist. Director: William Asher.
Darrin is arrested and accused of stealing the bed warmer.
Samantha learns that the bed warmer is actually a warlock who was transformed by Serena.

No. 205_____

Darrin on a Pedestal 10/22/70
GS: Robert Brown. Writer: Bernie Kahn. Director: William Asher.
Serena turns a Seaman's memorial statue to life and puts a petrified Darrin in its place.

No. 206_____

Paul Revere Rides Again 10/29/70
GS: Jonathan Harris, Bert Convy. Writer: Philip and Henry Sharp. Director: Richard Michaels.
Esmeralda accidentally conjures up Paul Revere.

No. 207_____

Samantha's Bad Day in Salem 11/5/70
GS: Hal England. Writer: Michael Morris. Director: William Asher.
A young warlock, who has a crush on Samantha, creates his own duplicate of her for himself, Larry Tate thinks it is Samantha. This causes problems for Darrin.

No. 208_____

Samantha's Old Salem Trip 11/12/70
GS: Ronald Long, James Westerfield. Writer: Ed Jurist. Director: William Asher.
Esmeralda accidentally sends Samantha back to 17th century Salem.

No. 209_____

Samantha's Pet Warlock 11/19/70
GS: Edward Andrew, Noam Pitlik. Writer: Jerry Mayer. Director: Richard Michaels.
An egotistical warlock tries to get Samantha to run away with him.

No. 210_____

Samantha's Old Man 12/3/70
GS: Ruth McDevitt. Writer: Ed Jurist. Director: Richard Michaels.
Endora turns Darrin into a seventy three year old man.

No. 211_____

The Corsican Cousins 12/10/70
GS: Barbara Morrison, Ann Doran, Robert Wolders. Writer: Ed Jurist. Director: Richard Michaels.
Endora casts a spell on Samantha and Serena, so that whatever one says the other will say and vice versa.

No. 212_____

Samantha's Magic Potion 12/17/70
GS: Charles Lane. Writer: Shirley Gordon. Director: Richard Michaels.
Samantha gives Darrin a magic potion, which will give him confidence.

No. 213_____

Sisters at Heart 12/24/70
GS: Don Marshall, Parley Baer. Written By: Thomas Jefferson High School Students, 5th Period English Class, 1970. Director: William Asher.
Tabitha causes polka dots to appear on herself and her black friend so they can both look-alike and be sisters.

No. 214 _____

The Mother-in-Law of the Year 1/14/71
GS: John McGiver, Jim Lange, Robert Q. Lewis. Writers: Philip and Henry Sharp. Director: William Asher.
Endora becomes the spokeswoman for bon bons when she is named Mother-in-Law of the year.

No. 215 _____

Mary, the Good Fairy (Part I) 1/21/71
GS: Imogene Coca, Ricky Powell. Writer: Ed Jurist. Director: William Asher.
The good fairy comes to collect Tabitha's lost tooth, but gets drunk on brandy when she takes it to cure her cold.

No. 216_____

The Good Fairy Strikes Again (Part II) 1/28/71
GS: Imogene Coca, Herb Voland, Vic Tayback, Paul Smith.
Writer: Ed Jurist. Director: William Asher.
Samantha tries to get the good fairy to take leave.

No. 217 _____

The Return of Darrin the Bold 2/4/71
GS: David Huddleston, Richard X. Slattery. Writer: Ed Jurist.
Director: Richard Michaels.
Serena goes back in time to the 14th century to visit Darrin's ancestor Darrin the
Bold, in order to turn him into a warlock, which in turn will cause Darrin to become a warlock also.

No. 218 _____

The House That Uncle Arthur Built 2/11/71
GS: Barbara Rhoades, Ysabel MacCloskey, J. Edward McKinley.
Writer: Bernie Kahn. Director: Richard Michaels.
Arthur transfers all of his practical jokes to the Stephens house so he will be able to hide his joking nature from a snobby witch he is dating.

No. 219 _____

Samantha and the Troll 2/18/71
GS: Bob Cummings, Felix Silla, Diane Murphy. Writers: Lila Garrett and Joel Rapp. Director: William Asher.
Tabitha brings her dolls to life, including a troll doll, which escapes.

No. 220

This Little Piggy 2/25/71
GS: Herb Edelman. Writer: Ed Jurist. Director: Richard Michaels.
Endora casts a spell on Darrin by giving him a pig's head.

No. 221 _____

Mixed Doubles 3/4/71
GS: Mitchell Silberman, Natalie Core. Writer: Richard Baer. Director: William Asher.
Samantha and Louise exchange personalities due to a metaphysical molecular disturbance.

No. 222 _____

Darrin Goes Ape 3/11/71
GS: Herb Vigran, Allen Jenkins, Milton Selzer. Writers: Leo and Pauline Townsend. Director: Richard Michaels.
Serena turns Darrin into an ape.

No. 223 _____

Money Happy Returns 3/18/71
GS: Arch Johnson, Karl Lukas, Allen Jenkings. Writer: Milt Rosen. Director: Richard Michaels.
Darrin finds a huge sum of money in the back of a cab.

No. 224 _____

Out of the Mouth of Babes 3/25/71
GS: David Huddleston, Gene Andrusco, Eric Scott. Writer: Michael Morris. Director: Richard Michaels.
Endora changes Darrin into a ten-year-old boy.

No. 225 _____

Samantha's Psychic Slip 4/1/71
GS: Irenee Byatt, Irwin Charone. Writer: John L. Greene. Director: William Asher.
Samantha finds that whenever she hiccups something disappears.

No. 226_____

Samantha's Magic Mirror 4/8/71
GS: Tom Bosley, Richard Rowley, Nancy Priddy. Writer: Ed Jurist. Director: Richard Michaels.
Esmeralda asks Samantha to help her with her magic so she can impress her boyfriend into marrying her.

No. 227_____

Laugh, Clown, Laugh 4/15/71
GS: Charles Lane, Ysabel MacCloskey, Marcia Wallace. Writer: Ed Jursit. Director: William Asher.
Endora casts a spell on Darrin, which causes him to constantly tell bad jokes.

No. 228_____

Samantha and the Antique Doll 4/22/71
Writer: Ed Jurist. Director: Richard Michaels.
Samantha tries to convince Darrin's mother that she has magical powers in order to cover up for Adam's witchcraft.

No. 229_____

How Not to Lose Your Head to Henry VIII (Part I)
9/15/71
GS: Ronald Long, Ivor Barry, Arlene Martel, Laurie Main. Writer: Ed Jurist. Director: William Asher.
Samantha is sent back in time to the court of Henry VIII when she helps a nobleman who was transformed into a painting by an evil witch.

No.230

How Not to Lose Your Head to Henry VIII (Part II)
9/22/71
GS: Ronald Long, Arlene Martel. Writer: Ed Jurist. Director: William Asher.
Endora sends Darrin back in time to rescue Samantha.

No. 231_____

Samantha and the Loch Ness Monster 9/29/71
GS: Steve Franken, Don Knight, Bernie Kopell. Writer: Michael Morris.
Director: William Asher.
The Loch Ness Monster wants Samantha to get Serena to turn him back into the warlock he was, until Serena changed him.

No. 232_____

Samantha's Not So Leaning Tower of Pisa 10/6/71
GS: John Rico, Robert Casper. Writer: Michael Morris.
Director: William Asher.
Esmeralda goes to Italy to straighten the Leaning Tower of Pisa, which she had caused to lean hundreds of years earlier.

No. 233_____

Bewitched, **Bothered and Baldoni** 10/13/71
GS: Francine York, Lou Krugman, Al Molinaro. Writer: Michael Morris.
Director: William Asher.
Endora causes the statue of Venus to come to life in order to cause trouble for Darrin.

138   The Magic of Bewitched Trivia

No. 234_____

Paris Witch's Style 10/20/71
GS: Maurice Marsac. Writer: Michael Morris. Director: William Asher. Maurice blames Darrin for not letting Samantha visit him while they were in London, so he sends him to the top of the Eiffel Tower.

No. 235_____

The Ghost Who Made a Spectre of Himself 10/27/71
GS: Patrick Horgan, Maurice Dallimore. Writer: Ed Jurist.
Director: William Asher.
While staying at a British castle, Darrin is possessed by a ghost who has fallen for Samantha.

No. 236_____

TV or Not TV 11/3/71
GS: Wanda Hendrix, Robert Q. Lewis, Roy R. Etherin, Kathleen Richards. Writer: Bernie Kahn. Director: William Asher.

No. 237_____

A Plague on Maurice and Samantha 11/10/71
GS: Bernie Kopell, Susan Hathaway, J. Edward McKinley.
Writer: Ed Jurist. Director: Richard Michaels.
Samantha loses her powers, and when Maurice kisses his daughter, he too loses his powers.

No. 238_____

Hansel and Gretel in Samanthaland 11/17/71
GS: Cindy Henderson, Eric Chase, Billie Hayes, Bobo Lewis.
Writer: Michael Morris. Director: Richard Michaels.
Tabitha changes places with Hansel and Gretel in her storybook, which causes Samantha to come after her.

No. 239_____

The Warlock in the Gray Flannel Suit 12/1/71
GS: Bernie Kopell, Charles Lane. Writer: John L. Greene.
Director: Richard Michaels.
Endora calls on a warlock to help get Darrin fired so Samantha can attend a wedding.

No. 240 _____

The Eight-Year-Itch Witch 12/8/71
GS: Julie Newmar. Writer: Ruth Brooks Flippen. Director: Richard Michaels.
Endora gets Ophelia, a cat, turned into a witch to help her make Samantha jealous.

No. 241 _____

Three Men and a Witch on a Horse 12/15/71
GS: John Fiedler, Scatman Crothers, Hoke Howell. Writer: Ed Jurist. Director: Richard Michaels.
Endora casts a spell on Darrin, turning him into a gambler.

No. 242 _____

Adam, Warlock or Washout 12/29/71
GS: Diana Cheshney, Maryester Denver, Bernie Kuby, Lew Horn. Writer: Ed Jurist. Director: William Asher.
Maurice tries to convince the witches council that Adam is a warlock.

No. 243 _____

Samantha's Magic Sitter 1/5/72
GS: Richard X. Slattery, Jeanne Arnold, Ricky Powell, Christian Juttner. Writers: Philip and Henry Sharp. Director: Richard Michaels.
Esmeralda baby-sits for the son of Darrin's client, which causes problems when the boy tells everyone that she is a witch.

No. 244 _____

Samantha Is Earthbound 1/15/72
GS: Jack Collins, Sara Seegar, Molly Dodd. Writer: Michael Morris. Director: Richard Michaels.
Samantha is suffering from a disease, which makes her very heavy, so as a cure Dr. Bombay makes her lighter than air until he can find a cure for her. Until then, Samantha has to find a way to keep herself from floating away.

No. 245_____

Serena's Richcraft 1/22/72
GS: Peter Lawford, Ellen Weston. Writer: Michael Morris.
Director: William Asher.
Serena loses her powers, so to make up for it she decides to romance a rich bachelor.
*Remake of Nos. 3 and 196.

No. 246_____

Samantha on Thin Ice 1/29/72
GS: Alan Oppenheimer, Bob Paul. Writer: Richard Baer.
Director: William Asher.
Endora turns Tabitha into a fantastic ice skater.

No. 247_____

Serena's Youth Pill 2/5/72
GS: David Hayward, Ted Foulkes, Irenee Byatt. Writer: Michael Morris. Director: E.W. Swackhamer.
Serena gives Larry a pill, which causes him to grow gradually younger by the minute.

No. 248_____

Tabitha's First Day at School 2/12/72
GS: Nita Talbot, Allen Jenkins, Maudie Prickett. Writer: Ed Jurist. Director: Richard Michaels.
Tabitha turns the class bully into a frog.

No. 249_____

George Washington Zapped Here (Part I) 2/19/72
GS: Will Geer, Jane Connell. Writer: Michael Morris.
Director: Richard Michaels.
Esmeralda accidentally zaps George Washington out of a book. When she tries to send him back, she zaps his wife Martha out of the book instead.

No. 250_____

George Washington Zapped Here (Part II) 2/26/72
GS: Will Geer, Jane Connell, Jack Collins. Writer: Michael Morris. Director: Richard Michaels.
George tries to help Darrin get a new client's account before he and Martha are returned to the book.

No. 251_____

School Days, School Daze 3/4/72
GS: Maudie Prickett, Charles Lane. Writer: Michael Morris.
Director: Richard Michaels.
Endora casts a spell, which turns Tabitha into a seven-year-old genius.

No. 252_____

A Good Turn Never Goes Unpunished 3/11/72
GS: J. Edward McKinley. Writer: Bernie Kahn. Director: Ernest Losso.
Darrin and Samantha fight over her use of witchcraft in trying to sell an ad campaign to a client.

No. 253_____

Sam's Witchcraft Blows a Fuse 3/18/72

GS: Bernie Kopell, Reta Shaw, Benson Fong, Janos Prohaska.
Writer: Leo Townsend. Director: Richard Michaels.
Samantha becomes affected by a drink in a Chinese restaurant. It causes her face to become covered with red stripes.

No. 254_____

The Truth, Nothing But the Truth, So Help Me, Sam
3/25/72
GS: Parley Baer, Sara Seegar. Writer: Ed Jurist. Director: William Asher.
Endora tests Darrin's love for Sam by bewitching a pin.

CHAPTER 5

Cosmic Connection

Show	Account	Accounts Client
3	Barker Baby Food	Rex Barker
5	Caldwell Soup	Phillip Caldwell
7	Halloween Candy	Mr. Brinkman
8	_____	Mr. Austen
11	Jasmine Perfume (Miss Jasmine Campaign)	_____
18	Margaret Marshall Cosmetics	_____
20	Woolfe Brothers Dept. Store	_____
21	Jewel of the East (jewelry)	Mr. Pickering
23	Slegershamer's Dairy	_____
30	Feather Touch Typewriters	_____
35	Perfect Pizza Parlors	Linton Baldwin
36	Shelley's Shoes	_____
38	Stanwyck Soap	Mr. Martin

41	E Z Open Flush Door	Mr. Foster
42	_____	Howard Norton
43	(Party Favors)	Jack Rogers
44	Mother Jenny's Jam	Charles Barlow
45	Jarvis Account; Slater; Murphy Supermarket	_____
46	Toy Ship Models	Mr. Harding
49	Harper's Honey	_____
50	Hotchkiss Appliance Co.	Ed Hotchkiss
52	Kingsley Potato Chips	_____
53	_____	H.J. Simpson
58	Hockestedder Toy Co.	_____
59	_____	Randolph Turgeon
60	Aubert of Paris	_____
	J.T. Glendon	_____
62	Naisley's Baby Food	_____
63	Westchester Consolidated Mills	James Robinson
64	Detergent	J.K. Kabaker
65	_____	Osgood Rightmire
66	Robbins Baby Food Co.	_____

67	Robbins Baby Food Co.	
68	Stern Chemical Co.	Sanford Stern
71	United Cosmetics	Tony Devlin
73	Waterhouse Thumbtack Co.	
75	Robbins Truck Transmissions	Mark Robbins
82	Wright Pens	
83	Macelroy Shoes	
85	_____	Randolph Parkinson, Jr.
86	_____	Max Cosgrove
87	Franklin Electronics	Bernie Franklin
89	Super Soapy Soap	Tom Scranton
92	Solow Toy Company	
93	Sheldrake Sausage	
94	Morton Milk	C.L. Morton
95	Ganzer Garage Doors	
96	Tropical Bathing Suits	
97	_____	Ed Pennybaker
98	Cunningham Perfume	
100	_____	Mr. Morgan
101	Warbell Dresses	Jay&Terry Warbell

102	Baldwin Blankets	Horace Baldwin
	Mayor Rocklin	Frank Eastwood
104	Madame Maruska Lipstick	_____
105	_____	client unnamed
106	Saunders Soups	_____
107	Hornbeck Pharmaceutical	_____
108	Rohrbach Steel Company	_____
109	_____	Bob Chase
110	Chef Romani Foods	_____
112	Bigelow Tires	_____
113	Carter Bros. Industrial Products (Anti-Smog Device)	_____
114	Baxter Sporting Goods	Joe Baxter
117	Springer Pet Foods	Alvin Springer
120	Gregson Home Appliances	_____
121	_____	Mr. Grayson
122	Chappell Baby Foods	Roy Chappell
123	Mortimer Instant Soups	Jesse Mortimer
124	Mint Brite Toothpaste	J.P. Pritchfield
125	Autumn Flame Perfume	Bo Callahan

126	Webley Foods	J.P. Sommers
127	Prune Valley Retirement Village	
		JonathanBrodhurst
		Leroy Wendell
128	Giddings Tractors	_____
129	Abigail Adams Cosmetics	Mr. Blumberg
132	_____	Dwight Sharpe
134	Baker Foods	Edgar Baker
136	Mishimoto TV Sets	Kensu Mishimoto
138	Omega National Bank	R.H. Markham
139	Hercules Tractors	Charles Gilbert
	Slocum Soup	OJ Slocum
	Angel Coffee	_____
146	Hascomb Drug Company	Whitney Hascomb
147	Zoom Detergent	H.L. Bradley
148	Barton Industries (Tinker Bell Diaper Division)	_____
149	E Z Way Rent A Car/ Save-Most Markets/ Mossler Enterprises	Harlan Mossler
152	_____	Mr. Stewart
153	Adrienne Sebastian Cosmetic Products _____	

155	Vino Vanita	Clio Vanita
157	"The Fuzzy Doll"	_____
	Hanley's Department Store	Jim Hanley
		Mr. Henderson
158	Dufee's Dog Food	Oscar Durfee
159	Campbell Sporting Goods	Waldo R. Campbell
160	Struthers Account	_____
162	Brawn Cologne	Evelyn Tucker
164	_____	J. Earl Rockeford
170	Bueno/aka Zap	Raul Garcia
172	Hampton Motors	_____
173	Top Tiger Cologne	Evelyn Charday
174	(A detergent account)	Mr. Paxton
175	Berkley Baby Food	_____
177	Bartenbach Beauty Products (Dental Cream, Hair Tonic, Wart Remover)	_____
178	_____	Alvin J. Sylvester
179	Illinois Meat Packers	_____
180	Bliss Pharmaceutical	Silas Bliss Sr. & Jr.
181	Bliss Pharmaceuticals	Silas Bliss Sr. & Jr.

183	Shotwell Pharmaceuticals	_____
185	Tanaka Electronics (Division of Tanaka Enterprises)	_____
187	Multiple Industries	H.B. Summers
189	_____	Mr. Nickerson
190	Top Pop	_____
191	Braddock Sporting Goods	Bob Braddock
192	Breeze Shampo	_____
194	Harrison Industries	John J. Harrison
195	A housing Development	_____
196	Dinsdale Soups	George Dinsdale
197	Barber Peaches	_____
199	Happy Heart Greeting Card	Augustus Sunshine
200	_____	George Meiklejohn
201	Gotham Industries	_____
202	_____	Ernest Hitchcock
205	Barrows Umbrellas	_____
206	British Imperial Textile Mills	Sir Leslie Bancroft
207	Blakely Account	_____
209	Gibbons Dog Burgers	Charles Gibbons

210	Beau Geste Toiletries	Jennings Booker
211	Bigelow Industries	J.J. Langley
212	Harmon Savings and Loan	_____
214	Bobbins Candy Bonbons/ Bobbins Buttery Bonbons	Bernard Bobbins
216	The Reducealator	Mr. Ferber
218	Rockfield Furniture	Lionel Rockfield
219	Berkley Hair Tonic	Roland Berkley
220	Colonel Brigham's Spareribs	Colonel Brigham
222	Cushman Cosmetics	_____
223	Patterson Account	_____
	Bradwell Account	_____
	Cushman's Restaurant	_____
224	Mother Flanagan's Irish Stew	Sean Flanagan
226	_____	Client in Chicago
227	Mount Rocky Mutual	Harold Jameson
232	Count Bracini's Olive Oil	_____
233	House of Baldoni	Ernesto Baldoni
234	Europa Tours	Henri Sagan
235	Regal Silverware	_____

236	Silverton Toy Company	Lester Silverton
237	Benson's Chili Con Carne	_____
239	Monticello Carpets	Mr. Cushman
240	Tom Cat Tractors Inc.	Mr. Burkeholder
241	_____	Mr. Spengler
243	_____	Elliott Norton
244	Prescott Shoes	Wilbur Prescott
245	Woolcott Towers	Harrison Woolcott
250	Whirlaway Washing Machines	Hector Jamison
252	Benson Sleep-Ezy Mattress	_____
253	Ah Fong's Restaurant	Mr. Fong
254	Cora May Sportswear	Cora May Franklin

Clients

Here is a listing of McMann & Tate Clients and how many times the actor appeared as a client on *Bewitched*:

J. Edward McKinley-9 times, Jack Collins-7, Charles Lane-7, Parley Baer-6, Irwin Charone-4, John Fiedler-4, Arthur Julian-4, Arch Johnson-4, Herb Voland-4, Larry D. Mann-3, Edward Andrews-2, John Gallaudet-2, George Ives-2, Nancy Kovack-2, Oliver McGowan-2, Cliff Norton-2, Mala Powers-2, Dan Tobin-2

Bewitching Fact:
Sara Seegar was a Client's wife 7 times.

In Episode #159, we find out that McMann & Tate has standing lunch reservations at The Golden Spoon Restaurant.

CHAPTER 6

Mangled Monikers

Darrin Name Quiz

Which Witch Called Darrin Which Name????

Can you pick the real names that Endora, Serena, Arthur, and Maurice Called Darrin Stephens?

1. Dalfin 2. Dumbo 3. Dudley 4. Darwin 5. Duncan 6. Dum-Dum 7. Dagwood 8. Dobbin 9. Durwood 10. Durweed 11. Darius 12. Dork 13. Dolby 14. Dalton 15. Dewey 16. Darwood 17. Donald 18. Dino 19. Durwin 20. Durward

Answers: Real names used by Sam's relatives included:
2. Dumbo, 4. Darwin, 6. Dum-Dum,
7. Dagwood, 9. Durwood, 16. Darwood

UNEARTHLY TERMINOLOGY

Here is a list of very popular *Bewitched* terms and their definitions.

Cloud #9—A retreat for Samantha's family.

Conjure-To make happen, to make visible.

Cosmos Cotillon—An annual dinner dance for witches and warlocks.

Dabbin-A name used by Endora to refer to Darrin (See also others listed below, plus try Darrin name quiz)

Darwood-A name used by Endora to refer to Darrin

Dobbin—A name used by Maurice to refer to Darrin.

Durweed-A name used by Endora to refer to Darrin (See also Durwood, What's his name, Dabbin, Darwood.)

Durwood-A name used by Endora to refer to Darrin.

Earthbound-When a witch or warlock is not able to use hers/his powers.

Grandmamma—The name Tabitha calls her Grandma Endora.

Grandpapa—The name Tabitha calls her Grandpa Maurice.

Groovy—A term used by Serena to mean hip.

Hip—A term used by Serena to mean cool, in with the times.

Incantation-Is a spell with rhymes and fancy terms.

Mortal—A mortal is a human, one without powers.

Sam—Nickname used to refer to Samantha, usually used by Darrin.

Sammy—Uncle Arthur uses this as a nickname to refer to Samantha.

Teleport-To move objects or people with the mind.

Twitch-A term used that means casting a spell, usually with a twitch of the nose.

Voracious Ravenousitis-A bug that affects witches and warlocks, causes an uncontrollable urge to eat.

Warlock—A male witch.

What's his name-A name used by Sam's family to refer to Darrin.

Wishcraft-A term usually used by young witches and warlocks, when they really want something badly it's called wishcraft.

Witches Council-The main governing body of all witches and warlocks, decides the rules and regulations.

Witchcraft—The ability to create magic. Samantha has promised Darrin That she will abstain from witchcraft.

Witches Honor—A witches oath to tell the truth.

Zap-A term used that means casting a spell.

FAMOUS LAST WORDS

"Ha ha ... ha-ha ... nothing"
—Dr. Bombay

"Abner, you won't believe what I saw Mrs. Stephens do!"
—Gladys Kravitz

"Paging Dr. Bombay, Emergency Come Right Away"
—Samantha, or Serena

"I think I'm going to fade."
—Esmeralda

"Next time, call through the exchange."

"Darrin, I have Mrs. Kravitz on line one."
—Betty, Darrin's secretary

"Darrin, I know you don't approve of witchcraft but it's what got you into this mess, so let it get you out of it."
—Samantha

"Oh Larry, I thought I saw Samantha turn herself into" ...
—Louise Tate

"You really did miss me, lets go home honey."
—Larry Tate

"Oh, dear!"
—Esmeralda

"Oh, my stars!"
—Samantha

"You think your wife is a witch, you ought to see my wife."
—Drunk at the bar

"Darrin, you are fired!"
—Larry Tate

"Like wow, totally groovy."
—Serena

"Mother you come here this instant! Mom?.... Mother?"
—Samantha

"I'm gonna count to three: One, two, three, four? five?"
—Samantha

"Don't forget Darrin we have a meeting tomorrow with the _____ account, so I'll see you bright eyed and bushy Tailed."
—Larry Tate

"Tate's the name, Advertising is my game."
—Larry Tate

"Sam don't talk to your mother that way."—Darrin to Samantha, a very unpredictable statement on Darrin's part, from Episode #17.

"I'm sorry Mr. _____, Darrin doesn't know what he's saying, he doesn't speak for the rest of us at McMann & Tate, as of now he's terminated."
—Larry Tate

"Well I kind of like Darrin's idea, it's original, unique, just the kind of thing we need at _____." (insert any account name)
—Client of McMann & Tate

"I'm going to have a sick headache."
—Mrs. Phyllis Stephens, Darrin's mother

"Gladys, are you sure you took your medication today?"
—Abner Kravitz

"I got mugged in the tunnel of love".—Abner Kravitz

"That's no woman, that's my mother-in-law."—Darrin Stephens

"Yagazuzie, yagazuzie, yagazuzuie, zim, zumazuzie, zumazuzie, zumazuzie, bim, hi!, zuma, hooga, pits!"-Darrin (recites this incantation thinking it will protect him from Endora)

"You're behaving exactly like a stereotype witch, and you are doing it to the one person who was willing to believe we're different."-Samantha to Endora, a turning point from Episode #43, "Trick or Treat", in which Samantha tries to get Endora to see that Darrin is willing to believe in them.

"I'll bet she has some strange disease and we could catch it. You want to wake up with something strange?"-Gladys to Abner, talking about Samantha Stephens
Abners response, "I've been doing that for twenty years!"

CHAPTER 7

Totally Trivia

ULTIMATE *BEWITCHED* EPISODE TRIVIA CHALLENGE

The Good Fairy Quiz from Episodes #215, 216

"When you have a job that you love ... you have to do it yourself!" **The Good Fairy**

Trivia Tidbit:
Imogene Cocoa

1) In episode 215, The Good Fairy makes a visit to the Stephen's household, what is the character's name?
   A. Alice
   B. Mary
   C. Esmeralda

2) Why does the Good Fairy pay the Stephen's a visit?
   _____

3) Name the actress who played the Good Fairy?
   _____

4) Why does the Good Fairy decide to give up her job?
   _____

5) Who took over the job of the Good Fairy?
   A. Endora
   B. Samantha
   C. Serena
   D. Esmeralda

6) In episode 216, "The Good Fairy Strikes Again," what is the name of the product that Darrin is trying to come up with a slogan for?
   A. Reducealator
   B. Zoom Detergent
   C. Berkley Hair Tonic

7) What is the product intended for?
   A. Get clothes whiter
   B. Assist in losing weight
   C. Make hair stay in place

Serena Stops The Show Episode 192

I'll Blow You A Kiss In The Wind
(by Tommy Boyce and Bobby Hart)

Whenever you are tonight
I got a feelin' that you look out of sight,
So I'm gonna blow you a kiss in the wind.

And when it reaches your lips your lips my dear,
You're gonna smile and feel me oh so near,
So I'm gonna low you a kiss in the wind.

I've been laying here in my bed
The images of pretty thoughts runnin' through my head
About a guy in my mind I can feel
I can almost touch
Oh, my goodness
I miss you and I want you so much.

Wherever you are tonight
I got a feelin' hat you look out of sight
So I'm gonna low you a kiss in the wind.
Yeah, I'm gonna blow you a kiss in the wind.

Photo provided by Mark Simpson.

1) In Episode 192 entitled," Serena Stops the Show," Serena wants a rock group to come sing at an event, name the group
   A. The Beatles
   B. The Monkees
   C. Tommy Boyce and Bobby Hart

2) Serena wants the mortal rock group sing at the?
   A. Galaxy Gala
   B. Cosmos Cotillion
   C. Cosmic Connection

3) What is this event for?
   A. Annual dinner dance
   B. Raise money for orphan witches and warlocks
   C. Chili Cook-off

4) Who participates in this event?
   _____

5) Serena approaches the duo, and asks them to sing at the event, they decline. She casts a spell on them, what does the spell do?
   _____

6) Name Serena's song?

Photo courtesy of the Mark Simpson Collection.
From Episode #245, "Serena's Richcraft".

Name the client of Darrin's that Serena spends quality time with?
a. Harrison Woolcott
b. Larry Woolcoat
c. Harley Davison

Who takes Serena's powers away?
a. Samantha
b. Endora
c. Contessa Piranha

Why are Serena's powers taken away?
a. Because Serena was being bossy
b. Because Serena got caught trying to steal someone's fiancé.
c. Because the Witches Council deemed it necessary.

Name credited for Serena in the closing credits?
a. Melody Johnson
b. Elizabeth Montgomery
c. Pandora Spocks

In which episode was Serena seen as a blonde.
a. Episode #245, "Serena's Richcraft"
b. Episode #111, Double, Double, Toil and Trouble".
c. Episode #217, "The Return of Darrin the Bold".

True/False

Serena's Richcraft is a remake of It Shouldn't Happen to a Dog.

Serena's Richcraft is a remake of A Chance on Love.

Serena replaces witchcraft with rich craft.

Peter Lawford played Serena's boyfriend in "Serena's Richcraft".

Serena is Samantha's cousin on her father's side.

Return of Darrin the Bold, Episode #217

"Night into day and day into night, back to the past with the speed of light, to Durwood the Bold to do this spell, I wish you luck, if not just yell."—Endora

1) Endora and Serena decide to transform Darrin into a
   _____

2) The spell requires Serena to go back to the
   A. Fourteenth Century
   B. Twelfth Century
   C. Thirteenth Century

3) What land must Serena travel to?
   A. England
   B. Scotland
   C. Norway
   D. Ireland

4) What does Serena need to do with Darrin the Bold's three beard hairs?
   _____

Tabitha's Very Own Samantha, Episode #189

Bewitching Fact:
In episode 189, "Tabitha's Very Own Samantha," Tabitha's chin is bandaged. Erin Murphy really hurt herself on a pony ride a few days earlier.

"I wish, I wish, I wish I had my very own special mommy that I don't have to share with anyone."
—Tabitha

"Women become difficult early in life"-Darrin (referring to Tabitha's tantrum)

"Have a nice long rest".—Gladys Kravitz
"What for, there's nothing wrong with me?"—Samantha
"That's what they all say!"—Gladys Kravitz

In this episode, Gladys Kravitz asks who she thinks is Samantha, "Where is the baby?" Tabitha's very own Samantha responds, "What baby?"

1) Why is Tabitha upset?
    A. Because Samantha will not allow Tabitha to attend a trip to the moon with her grandmamma, Endora
    B. Because Tabitha has to share Samantha with Adam
    C. She didn't get to play with Gladys' nephew Sidney

True/False
2) Serena dresses up and plays Samantha for the day at her nieces request.

3) Tabitha uses a _____ spell to conjure up her own mother.

4) What is special about Tabitha's copy of Samantha?
   _____

5) Where does the duplicate Samantha take Tabitha?
    A. To the zoo
    B. To the amusement park
    C. To the shopping mall

6) Who encounters Tabitha and the duplicate Samantha?
   A. Larry Tate
   B. Phyllis Stephens
   C. Gladys Kravitz

European Vacation

Like in the 7th season when *Bewitched* went on location to Salem, Massachuttes,the cast and crew decided to take the show in its' last season to the beautiful and majestic location of Europe.

1) In Episode #230, Samantha gets zapped back to the court of
   _____.

2) What funny noise does Endora tell Darrin to do to get her attention If he needs help?
   A. Bark
   B. Quack
   C. Sneeze

3) In Episode #231, "Samantha and the Loch Ness Monster", Darrin And Samantha are in:
   A. England
   B. Scotland
   C. Italy

4) The Loch Ness Monster is actually a warlock named:
   A. Kevin
   B. David
   C. Bruce

5) Who had turned the warlock into the Loch Ness Monster?
   A. Endora
   B. Esmeralda
   C. Serena

6) In Episode #232, "Samantha's Not-So-Leaning Tower of Pisa", who was responsible for making the tower lean?
   A. Endora
   B. Clara
   C. Esmeralda

7) How does she make it lean?
   A. She zaps up a "lean" sandwich for her boyfriend
   B. She is doing a dance
   C. She gets mad, and makes it lean

8) True/False Samantha brings to life the statue of Venus?

9) True/False Endora brings to life the statue of Adonis?

10) Why are the statue/s brought to life in Episode #233, "Bewitched, Bothered, and Baldoni?"

___

11) Who gets into trouble in Episode #235, "The Ghost Who Made *a* Specter of Himself?"
   A. Darrin
   B. Larry
   C. Louise

12) Darrin is accused of:
   A. Stealing
   B. Being a Ghost
   C. Flirting with Louise

Gina Meyers 173

IT'S ALL RELATIVE

1. Darrin has an aunt who is mentioned, but never seen. Name her.
   A. Madge
   B. Midge
   C. Mary

2. Darrin and Samantha's offspring are:
   A. Erin and Greg
   B. Cindy, Jan, and Marsha
   C. Tabitha and Adam

3. Who is Samantha's great aunt?
   A. Clara
   B. Esmeralda
   C. Cornelia

4. _____ is Darrin's grandfather.
   A. Ernie
   B. Bert
   C. Grover

5. _____ is Darrin's great aunt (by blood, not by marriage)
   A. Helen
   B. Emma
   C. Tabitha

6. Which of Samantha's aunts is mentioned, but not seen on the series.
   A. Clara
   B. Bertha
   C. Agnes

7. True/False) Edgar is Samantha's elf cousin.

8. True/False) Arthur is Maurice's brother.

9. True/False) Panda is Samantha's cousin that is mentioned.

10. Darrin the _____ is an ancestor of the Stephens family.
    A. Bold
    B. Greek
    C. Tired

11. Which of the following three people is Samantha's second cousin?
    A. Lucretia
    B. Lorenzo
    C. Mario

12. _____ is Samantha's relaive on Maurice's side?
   A. Arthur
   B. Emma
   C. Serena

WIVES

Furnish the husband's name for each wife.

1. Samantha Stephens _____

2. Gladys Kravitz _____

3. Louise Tate _____

4. Phyllis Stephens _____

5. Endora _____

Cosmic Characteristics

Furnish the character's name for each description.

1. Bumbling, senile, well meaning _____

2. Noisy neighbor _____

3. Wallflower, shy, clumsy _____

4. Quack _____

5. Trickster, prankster _____

6. Flaky, hypocritical _____

7. Hypochondriac _____

8. Conniver, meddler _____

9. Hippy, groovy _____

10. Shakespeare lover _____

Gina Meyers

Which Witch Is Which?

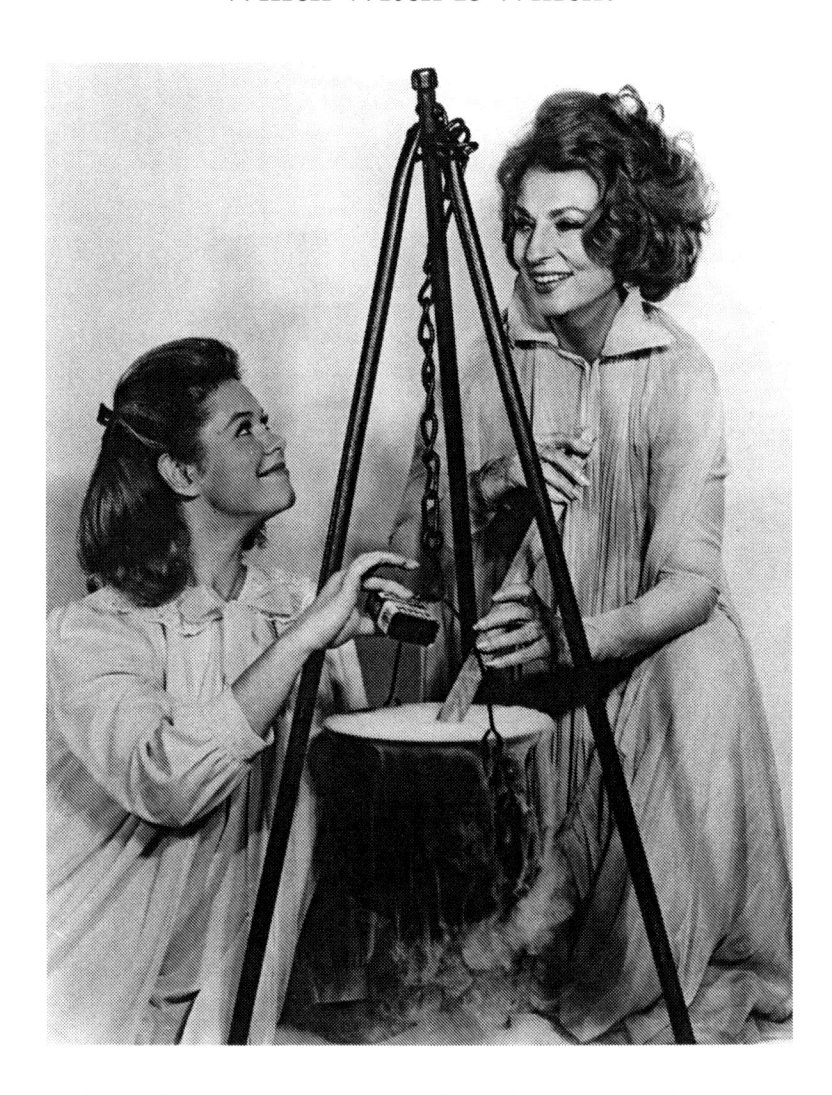

Classify the characters as either mortal, witches, or warlocks

1. Tabitha Stephens _____

2. Gladys Kravitz _____

3. Abner Kravitz _____

4. Maurice _____

5. Dr. Bombay _____

6. Darrin Stephens _____

7. Adam Stephens _____

8. Serena _____

9. Uncle Arthur _____

10. Esmeralda _____

11. Frank Stephens _____

12. Phyllis Stephens _____

13. Howard McMann _____

14. Aunt Hagatha _____

15. Aunt Clara _____

16. Louise Tate _____

17. Endora _____

18. Larry Tate _____

19. Samantha Stephens_____

20. Aunt Enchantra _____

21. The Apothecary _____

22. Betty, the secretary _____

WHO SAID IT?

"Tabitha must not twitch!" _____

"Abner, there she goes again, I just saw Samantha Stephen's turn a man into a frog!" _____

"His honor is as true in this appeal as thou art all unjust." _____

"Darrin, I hate to have to do this to you, but you're fired!" _____

"Hey now that's pretty hip." _____

"Weeell …" _____

"It's impossible to carry on a successful relationship with someone that's 95% water!" _____

"It's impossible to carry on a successful relationship with something that's 100% hot air!" _____

"Ooooh no, I think I'm going to fade." _____

"I think I'm going to have one of my sick headaches!" _____

"You Son of a Gun" _____

"Hiya Sammy!" _____

"Oh, my Stars!" _____

"Hello, tall, dark, and Nothing!" _____

THE *BEWITCHED* PUZZLE

1. Spin-off from *Bewitched* called _____

2. Adam to Tabitha _____

3. He played Larry Tate _____

4. Darrin's mother _____

5. Abner's spouse _____

6. Darrin's secretary _____

7. Endora to Darrin _____

8. Endora and Samantha often visited Cloud # _____

9. Name credited for Elizabeth Montgomery's portrayal of Serena _____

10. He played Samantha's dad _____

11. Samantha wiggled her _____

12. She played the role of Phyllis Stephens _____

13. Darrin's line of work _____

14. Dick York and Dick Sargent _____

15. Serena to Samantha _____

16. Samantha and Darrin were portrayed in this stone age cartoon _____

17. Samantha Stephens nickname _____

18. Maurice to Endora _____

19. Darrin's' Boss _____

20. Larry Tate's partner _____

21. City Darrin worked in _____

22. Samantha Stephens eye color is _____

BEWITCHED STARS

Match the actors name with the role they played.

Role   **Played By**

1. Orson Welles' mother in Citizen Kane _____

2. Mrs. Gurney from Mr. Peepers _____

3. Tom Colwell from Going My Way_____

4. Lt. Maxwell Trotter from Broadside _____

5. Regular on Hollywood Squares _____

6. Bernice Clifton from Designing Women _____

7. The Ships doctor from The Love Boat _____

8. Regular on The Jonathan Winter's Show _____

    Dick York
    Dick Sargent
    Marion Lorne
    Agnes Moorehead
    Paul Lynde
    Bernie Kopell
    Alice Ghostley
    Dick York

The Bewitching Hour Questions

1. What network did *Bewitched* air on? _____

2. How many seasons was *Bewitched* on? _____

3. Dick Sargent changed his name from? _____

4. Which actress on *Bewitched* co-starred in Citizen Kane a few years earlier? _____

5. What was the Stephen's address? _____

6. What was the name of Larry and Louise Tate's son? _____

7. What was Endora's brothers name? _____

8. Who was the older sibling Adam or Tabitha? _____

9. What did Tabitha call Endora? _____

10. What did Tabitha call Phyllis Stephens? _____

11. Elizabeth Montgomery is the child of a famous actor, name him. _____

12. At the end of the 1968-69 season there was a major change that took place yet it wasn't announced, what was it? _____

13. How did most of Darrin's advertising slogans originate? _____

14. What was the first telecast date of *Bewitched*?
_____

15. What was the last telecast date of *Bewitched*?
_____

16. What did Gladys Kravitz always try to convince her husband Abner of?

17. What year and month was Tabitha born in?

18. Name the main governing body of all the witches and warlocks?

19. How did Tabitha do witchcraft?

20. What does witches honor mean?

21. How was the sign for witches honor done?

22. Who did Tabitha call Grandpapa?

23. In one episode, Tabitha conjured up a Macedonian Dodo bird. Endora developed an allergy to the bird, what happened?

24. In the *Jack and The Beanstock* episode, Tabitha decided that her parents liked boys better than girls so she ran away from home. Can you name the famous football player who made his TV debut as the guard to the Beanstock?

25. Can you name the actor who played the occasional role as the warlock apothecary? *Hint: He was famous for his role as the ships doctor on *The Love Boat*.

26. Who was Larry Tate always trying to impress?

184   The Magic of Bewitched Trivia

27. Larry called Darrin a creative _____

28. What was the name of Sam's family physician?
    _____

29. Where did Dr. Bombay take Sam's pulse?
    _____

30. Whenever Esmeralda got embarrassed, what happened?
    _____

31. What was wrong with Aunt Clara?
    _____

32. Endora wanted the Witches Council to rule and make Aunt Clara
    _____

33. When Endora would promise Samantha not to interfere with Darrin, who would she get to do her dirty work?
    _____

34. Abner Kravitz sister's name was _____

35. Besides just playing Samantha Stephens, Elizabeth Montgomery also played another part. Who did she play?
    _____

36. What was Mr. McMann's first name? _____

37. What was Mr. McMann's wife's name? _____

38. What was the name of the actress who played Mrs. McMann? _____

39. When Darrin would get really upset, he would retreat to the local
    _____

40. What did Maurice call Darrin?_____

41. What did Darrin call Dr. Bombay? _____

42. Gladys Kravitz had a nephew, name him. _____

43. What was the name of the Real Estate company that the Stephen's purchased their home from? _____

44. What was the Stephen's home phone number? _____

45. What was Darrin's work number at McMann and Tate? _____

46. What was Darrin's license plate number? _____

47. In the French translation of *Bewitched*, what did they call Darrin? _____

48. What did Uncle Arthur call Samantha? _____

49. Did Endora ever get Darrin's name right? _____

50. Can you recite the *Bewitched* theme lyrics? _____

51. Darrin had an aunt that thought she was a lighthouse, what was her first name? _____

52. In 192, "Serena Stops the Show", what was the name of Serena's song? _____

53. What was the day, month, and year of Darrin and Samantha's first date? _____

54. What was the name of the Restaurant that Darrin and Samantha ate at on their first date? _____

55. Name the High Priestess of Witchdom. _____

56. *Bewitched* was a _____ Production.

57. Name the creator of *Bewitched*. _____

58. One of Darrin's favorite dishes is Beef _____

59. Name Darrin's ancestor _____.

60. What floor is Darrin's office located on? _____

61. What was Darrin's grandfather's name? _____

62. What was the name of the building that Darrin works in?
_____

63. Name one main commercial sponsor of *Bewitched*?
_____

64. Name the Queen of all the Witches?
_____

65. Elizabeth Montgomery had an unusual ability to wiggle her _____.

HIS OR HERS

Down below is a list of names. Select the individual as either Samantha's relative, Darrin's relative, or neither.

Endora _____

Aunt Clara _____

Maurice _____

Hepzibah _____

Serena _____

Cousin Henry _____

Cousin Helen _____

Aunt Hagatha _____

Betty _____

Dr. Bombay _____

Jon Tate _____

Gladys Kravitz _____

Cousin Edgar _____

Sidney Kravitz _____

Apothecary _____

There are six neither in the above His or Hers section, now list who they are and who their characters were on *Bewitched*.

1. _____

2. _____

3. _____

4. _____

5. _____

6. _____

Easy Multiple Choice

1. What did Endora call Darrin?
    A. Dabin
    B. Durweed
    C. Darwood
    D. All of the above

2. In the last season of the show, the *Bewitched* cast packed their bags and headed for.
   A. Hawaii
   B. Europe
   C. California
   D. Australia

3. Samantha's mothers name is?
   A. Esmeralda
   B. Endora
   C. Enchantra
   D. The wicked witch of the North

4. What was Darrin Stephen's profession?
   A. He is a professional golfer
   B. He is a marketing executive
   C. He is an astronaut
   D. He is an advertising executive

5. What seemed to be a main source of relief for Darrin after a hectic day at work and from battling witchcraft?
   A. He usually goes to sleep
   B. He reads a book
   C. He watches television
   D. He stays at home and has a drink

6. What did Darrin want Sam to give up?
   A. Smoking
   B. Witchcraft
   C. Working
   D. None of the above

7. What were the Stephen's two favorite drinks?
   A. Margaritas
   B. Scotch and water
   C. Martini with olives
   D. Pina coladas

8. Darrin had an aunt that was mentioned, but never seen. She thought she was?
   A. Lighthouse
   B. A Lamp
   C. Betsy Ross
   D. A Car

9. Where did Darrin work at?
   A. McMann, Tate, and Stephens
   B. McMann and Tate
   C. Hopkins Realty Company
   D. None of the above

10. Endora's friends were?
    A. Enchantra
    B. Esmeralda
    C. Hagatha
    D. Enchantra and Hagatha

11. In 1969, the Stephen's got a housekeeper, what was her name?
    A. Alice
    B. Clara
    C. Enchantra
    D. Esmeralda

12. A popular magazine in January of 1965 said this of Samantha Stephen's, "She is hem-deep in ticky-tacky, a clean-scrubbed, suburban Everywoman, with her caldron hooked to the rotisserie." Can you name the magazine that this quote was taken from?
    A. *Look*
    B. *Life*
    C. *Good Housekeeping*
    D. *Time*

13. Name the Avenue that Darrin worked on?
    A. 5th Avenue
    B. Madison Avenue
    C. New York Street
    D. 6th Avenue

14. What college did Darrin attend?
    A. Arizona State
    B. Ohio State
    C. Missouri State
    D. Mississippi State

15. Serena's pet name for Larry Tate was
    A. Snowman
    B. Cotton Ball
    C. Peter Rabbit
    D. Peter Cotton Top

16. What is Samantha and Darrin's favorite Holiday?
    A. Easter
    B. Christmas
    C. Thanksgiving
    D. Halloween

17. What is Endora's favorite Holiday?
    A. Thanksgiving
    B. National Witches Day
    C. Halloween
    D. None of the above

18. Which witch-disease did Samantha not contract.
    A. Gravititus Inflammities
    B. Vocabularyitis
    C. Voracious ravenousitis
    D. Molecular metaphysical disturbance

19. What does Clara enjoy collecting?
    A. Doorknobs
    B. Cats
    C. Fishhooks
    D. Boyfriends

… And the Emmy Goes to:

20. Bewitched received _____ Emmys?
    A. 3
    B. 8
    C. 22

21. How many times was Bewitched nominated for an Emmy?
    A. 2
    B. 22
    C. 222

Mothers'-In-Law

22. Who is Phyllis jealous of in Episode # 182, "Sam's Double Mother Trouble?"
    A. Mother Goose
    B. Mary, Mary Quite Contrary
    C. Queen Victoria

23. Name the restaurant that Samantha and Endora try to help publicize in Episode #35?
    A. Luigis
    B. Marios
    C. Louies

24. Phyllis often gets?
    A. Sick headaches
    B. Hemorrhoids
    C. Diarrhea

25. Bewitched was on for how many seasons?
    A. eight
    B. six
    C. ten

Groovy, Groovy, just for Fun, You decide:

As we all know, Serena liked to be the center of attention. If she pursued a career in the mortal realm, what do you think she would have chosen? Submit your answers to www.magicofbewitched.com. Your answers may be used in an upcoming edition.

Black Magic
Lisa Hartman is married to
Country Music Singer, Clint Black.

TABITHA COMEDY TRIVIA

1. What was the official first telecast date of Tabitha?
   _____

2. What was the last telecast date of Tabitha?
   _____

3. What was Tabitha a spin-off from?
   _____

4. What network did Tabitha air on?
   _____

5. Who played the role of Tabitha Stephens?
   _____

6. Who played the role of Adam Stephens?
   _____

7. Where did Tabitha work and what did she do?
   _____

8. What was the name of Tabitha's meddlesome Aunt?
   _____

9. Why wasn't Erin Murphy asked to play the part of Tabitha?
   _____

10. What city and state was Tabitha situated in?
    _____

11. What was the name of Tabitha's boss?
    _____

12. How did Tabitha get herself out of bad situations?
    _____

13. Who sang the theme song in the opening sequence of Tabitha?
    _____

14. Who was Paul Thurston?
   _____

15. How many seasons was Tabitha on for?
   _____

16. Who was the director for the Tabitha series?
   _____

17. Which actress played Tabitha in the pilot show?
   _____

18. What type of car did Tabitha drive in the opening credits?
   _____

19. What color was Tabitha's car in the opening sequence?
   _____

CAST:

ROLE	PLAYED BY
Tabitha Stephens	Lisa Hartman
Paul Thurston	Robert Urich
Marvin Decker	Mel Stewart
Adam Stephens	David Ankrum
Aunt Minerva	Karen Morrow

Bewitched Tabitha spin-off Episode Titles

Pilot directed by Bruce Bilson
The Halloween Episode
Tabitha's Weighty Problem
A Star Is Born
Tabitha's Triangle
Minerva Goes Straight
Mr. Nice Guy
The Arrival of Nancy
The New Black Magic
What's Wrong with Mr. Right?
Paul Goes to New York
Tabitha's Party

I Dream of Jeannie Déjà vu Trivia Questions

Extreme Home Makeover Trivia:
   In the episode "Hippie, Hippie, Hooray", we see Larry and Louise Tate in their kitchen. It's the same set used as Tony Nelson's kitchen from "I Dream of Jeannie".

1. _____ network countered by introducing a pretty blonde _____ named _____.

2. Jeannie's last name was _____.
    A. Hagman
    B. Evans
    C. Nelson

3. For the duration of *I Dream of Jeannie*, what did Jeannie attempt to do with Tony?
    A. Get him to marry her.
    B. Get him into trouble.
    C. Teach her how to cook.

4. Tony's friend Roger knew Jeannie was a Genie?
    A. True
    B. False

5. Who is Dr. Alfred Bellows?
    A. Gladys Kravitz cousin
    B. Ship's doctor
    C. Psychiatrist at Captain Nelson's base.

6. Jeannie's twin sister's name is:
    A. Pandora Spocks
    B. Jeannie, bien sur
    C. Serena

Tabitha Stephens Trivia

Tabitha Tidbit
The name Tabatha appears in the Old Testament.

Erin Murphy will tour the Warner Brothers lot in the upcoming *Bewitched* on DVD box set.

Beginning in Episode #171, "Sam and the Beanstalk", Tabitha is spelled with an "I", as previously it had been spelled Tabatha with an "a".

1. Tabitha was born on the telecast on
   a. January 13, 1966
   b. October 31, 1966
   c. June 6, 1966

2. Tabitha was born at _____ hospital.
   a. St. Agnes
   b. St. Luke's
   c. Perkins

3. Who came up with the name Tabitha?
   a. Samantha
   b. Serena
   c. Endora

4. The name Tabitha in Arabic means:
   a. Happy
   b. Pretty
   c. Gazelle

5. Which set of twins took over the role of Tabitha as a toddler?
   a. Heidi and Laura Gentry
   b. Tamara and Julie Young
   c. Erin and Diane Murphy

6. Who later resumed the role of Tabitha entirely?
   a. Erin Murphy
   b. Tamara Young
   c. Julie Young

7. Name Tabitha's first pediatrician
   a. Dr. Koblin
   b Dr. McDonald
   c. Dr. Donald

8. Tabitha's favorite dessert is:
   a. chocolate pudding
   b. raisin cookies
   c. chocolate donuts

9. Darrin discovers that Tabitha is a witch in Episode # ___.

   a. Episode #76, "The Moment of Truth"
   b. Episode #54, "And Then There Were Three"
   c. He never finds out

10. In Episode #178, "A Bunny For Tabitha", who brings Tabitha a wish box as her birthday present?
    a. Maurice
    b. Uncle Arthur
    c. Serena

In Episode #151, "I Don't Want To Be a Toad", Tabitha goes to _____ School. Her friend _____ doesn't want to be a _____, so Tabitha Transforms her into a _____.
Their teacher Mrs. Birch thinks she has ____
Her student. After this incident, they decide to _____ the school.

Romancing Taking Flight, Samantha and Darrin Trivia

1. In Episode #1, "I, Darrin, Take This Witch Samantha", it is revealed that Samantha and Darrin meet while
   A. Walking
   B. Going through a revolving door
   C. Running

2. Name the city where Samantha and Darrin meet for the first time.
   A. New York City
   B. Chicago
   C. Atlantic City

3. It is revealed in Episode #198, "Mona Sammy", that Samantha wore this on their first date.
   A. a Pink Pokka Dot Dress
   B. a Pink wool dress
   C. a baby blue overcoat

4. In Episode #97, "I Remember You Sometimes", Darrin brings Samantha flowers to celebrate the anniversary of:
   A. their first meeting
   B. their first wedding anniversary
   C. their first quarrel.

5. In Episode #37, "Alias Darrin Stephens", Darrin gives Samantha a/an _____ as a present.
   A. Heart Shaped necklace
   B. A Watch
   C. A diamond ring

6. In Episode #171, "Sam and the Beanstock", it is mentioned that Samantha and Darrin have settled on what names for the upcoming birth of the baby.
   A. Adam and Tabitha
   B. Elizabeth and William
   C. James and Susan

7. Where do Sam and Darrin have their first date?
   A. Sorrento's Restaurant
   B. Mario's Restaurant
   C. Laundromat

8. From Episode #1, Samantha and Darrin meet:
   A. through a mutual friend
   B. at a sock hop
   C. Walking through a revolving door.

9. Darrin's ex-girlfriends' name is:
   A. Brenda
   B. Sheila
   C. Sally

10. What does Darrin's ex-girlfriend do to Samantha?
    A. She tells Samantha to dress casually to a dinner party
    B. She asks Samantha to bring a friend to the dinner party
    C. She asks Samantha to bring a Jell-O salad to the dinner party

11. In Episode #44, what happens to Darrin and Samantha's clothing?
    A. It shrinks
    B. It disappears
    C. It is automatically sent to the dry cleaners

12. Who accidentally does this to Samantha and Darrin's clothes?
    A. Esmeralda
    B. Endora
    C. Clara

Witches and Warlocks are my Favorite Things Trivia

Gina Meyers looking into a mirror. Photo courtesy of David Lawrence Meyers.
Vanity Faire Tidbit:
Esmeralda wanting to be younger zaps all the mirrors in the Stephens household to make herself look younger and prettier. Tom Bosley from Happy Days fame plays in Episode #226, "Samantha's Magic Mirror".

Trivia Tidbit:
Alice Ghostley first appeared on *Bewitched* as a clumsy and ditsy maid named Naomi in "Maid to Order", she takes over for the the Tate's' sick maid who is referred to as Esmeralda.

1. Who uses the magic phrase "Zolda pranken kopek lum" from Episode #7, "The Witches Are Out"?
   A. Esmeralda
   B. Bertha
   C. Endora

2. The Witches Convention is officially known as:
   A. The Interplanetary Warlock Club
   B. The Centennial Convocation of the Witches of the World
   C. The Cosmos Cotillion

3. The office of the Resident Witch of Salem was established in 1692 by:
   A. High Priestess Hepzibah
   B. Endora
   C. Aunt Clara

4. What does the magic phrase, "Ahmed Talu Varsi Lupin", from Episode #208, "Samantha's Old Salem Trip" mean in ancient Babylonian?
   A. Best wishes
   B. Bon Voyage
   C. Good luck

5. Sometimes witches notify Samantha of important news via a flaming spear, also known as:
   A. A Witch-O-Gram
   B. A Teleport
   C. A Spearhead

6. In Episode #125, "Once in a Vial", Samantha is invited to the Cosmos Cotillion by who courtesy of whom?
   A. Rollo, Endora
   B. George, Endora
   C. Rollo, Maurice

7. In Episode #239, "The Warlock in the Gray Flannel Suit", Samantha's cousin _____ is getting married.
   A. Pandora
   B. Panda
   C. Samsara

8. Also from Episode #239, "The Warlock in the Gray Flannel Suit", Endora mentions that the wedding will be held in:
   A. Paris
   B. Hong Kong
   C. London

9. Who did Samantha bring home when she was a little girl, according to episode #204?
   A. Queen Victoria
   B. Sir Walter Raleigh
   C. Robin Hood

Extreme Home Makeover Trivia

The exterior of the Kravitz house is the same exterior as used in "Partridge Family", as well as "The Donna Reed Show".

Trivia Tidbit:

Endora decides to host a wild Halloween party in the Stephens' home. Uncle Arthur and Samantha try to move the party to an alternative location, which ignites a spar between Arthur and Endora.

1. The *Bewitched* Home was used on other Columbia Studio television series. Which series was the *Bewitched* house not featured in?
   A. *I Dream of Jeannie*
   B. *All In The Family*
   C. *The Donna Reed Show*

2. In Episode #81, "The House That Uncle Arthur Built", what keeps happening to the house?
   A. It keeps appearing and disappearing.
   B. Councilman Green believes it to be the world's thinnest house on earth.
   C. Endora keeps redecorating the home.

3. In Episode #126, "Snob In The Grass", what do the Stephens have installed?
   A. New plumbing
   B. A new roof
   C. New Sprinklers

4. The Stephens live at:
   A. 1313 Mockingbird Lane
   B. 1164 Morning Glory Circle
   C. 158 Elm Street

5. What city and state is *Bewitched* situated in?
   A. Salem, Massachusetts
   B. Westport, Connecticut
   C. Ithaca, New York

6. Name the Realty Company that represents the Stephen's home?
   A. Westport Realty
   B. Hopkins Realty
   C. Pearson Realty

7. In Episode 201, Samantha and Darrin's bathroom gets a makeover. What are the color of the walls?
   A. Blue
   B. Green
   C. Purple

8. In Episode #116, what color are the tiles in the bathroom?
   A. Green and White tiles
   B. Orange and Green tiles
   C. Purple and Blue tiles

9. What color is Tabitha's Nursery, as seen in Episode #75, "Nobody's Perfect".
   A. Blue
   B. Yellow
   C. Pink

10. In Episode #241, "Three Men and a Witch on a Horse", Tabitha's big girl room is accented with what color?
    A. Green
    B. Yellow
    C. Pink

11. What happens in Episode #131, "How Green Was My Grass"?
    A. Darrin thinks Samantha has conjured up synthetic grass in the front yard.
    B. Darrin thinks Samantha has placed new real grass in the front yard.
    C. Samantha thinks Darrin has replaced the grass in the front yard.

12. In Episode #2, "Be It Ever So Mortgaged", Samantha tries to prove to Endora that
    A. Cloud 9 is perfect in the summer.
    B. Going to Rome sounds fun!
    C. A new home is a nice place to live.

ANSWERS

Ultimate Bewitched Episode Trivia Challenge
The Good Fairy Quiz Answers:

1. B. 2; Tabitha has lost her tooth; 3. Imogene Cocoa; 4.She is tired; 5. B.; 6. A.; 7.B.

Serena Stops the Show Quiz

1. C.; 2. B. Cosmos Cotillion; 3. A. An Annual dinner dance; 4. Witches and warlocks; 5. Makes them unpopular, 6. "I'll Blow You a Kiss in the Wind."

Serena's Richcraft Quiz:

Harrison Woolcott, c. Contessa Piranha, b. Because Serena got caught trying to steal someone's boyfriend, C. Pandora Spocks, A. "Double, Double, Toil, and Trouble". True, True, True, True, True.

Return of Darrin The Bold Quiz

1. Warlock; 2. A; 3. B; 4. Mixes a sample of his hair into a witch's formula.

Tabitha's Very Own Samantha Quiz

1. B.; 2. False; 3. Wishcraft; 4. She gives Tabitha undivided attention, 5. B; 6.C

European Vacation answers:

1. Henry VIII, 2. B., 3. B., 4. C., 5. C., 6.C., 7. A., 8. False, 9. False, 10. To test Darrin's love for Samantha, 11. A., 12. C.

IT'S ALL RELATIVE ANSWERS:

1. A. Madge; 2. C. Tabitha and Adam; 3. C. Cornelia; 4. C. Grover; 5. B. Emma; 6. C. Agnes; 7. True; 8. False; 9. True; 10. A. Bold; 11. A. Lucretia; 12. C. Serena

WIVES:

1. Darrin Stephens
2. Abner Kravitz

3. Larry Tate
4. Frank Stephens
5. Maurice

Cosmic Characteristics:

1. Aunt Clara
2. Gladys Kravitz
3. Esmeralda
4. Dr. Bombay
5. Uncle Arthur
6. Larry Tate
7. Phyllis Stephens
8. Endora
9. Serena
10. Maurice

Which Witch Is Which?

1. Witch
2. Mortal
3. Mortal
4. Warlock
5. Warlock
6. Mortal
7. Warlock
8. Witch
9. Warlock
10. Witch
11. Mortal
12. Mortal
13. Mortal
14. Witch
15. Witch
16. Mortal
17. Witch
18. Mortal
19. Witch
20. Witch
21. Warlock
22. Mortal

Who Said It?

Samantha or Darrin
Gladys Kravitz
Maurice
Larry Tate
Serena
Samantha
Endora
Darrin
Esmeralda
Phyllis Stephens
Larry Tate
Uncle Arthur
Samantha
Serena

Bewitched Puzzle:

1. Tabitha
2. Brother
3. David White
4. Phyllis Stephens
5. Gladys Kravitz
6. Betty
7. Mother-in-law
8. Nine or eight
9. Pandora Spocks
10. Maurice Evans
11. Nose
12. Mabel Albertson
13. Advertising
14. Darrin Stephens
15. Cousin
16. Flintstones
17. Sam or Sammy
18. Husband
19. Larry Tate/and or Howard McMann
20. Howard McMann
21. Manhattan
22. Green

Answers: *Bewitched* Stars

1. Agnes Moorehead
2. Marion Lorne
3. Dick York
4. Dick Sargent
5. Paul Lynde
6. Alice Ghostley
7. Bernie Kopell
8. Alice Ghostley or Paul Lynde

Answers to: The Bewitching Hour:

1. ABC, 2. Eight, 3. Wally Cox, 4. Agnes Moorehead, 5. 1164 Morning Glory Circle, 6. Jon, 7. Arthur, 8. Tabitha, 9. Grandmamma, 10. Grandma Stephens, 11. Robert Montgomery, 12. Dick York was replaced by Dick Sargent, 13. Witchcraft, 14. September 17, 1964 15. July 1, 1972, 16. That Samantha is a witch, 17. January 13, 1966, 18. Witches Council, 19. Put her finger on her nose, 20. Oath, promise,

21. Placing index and middle in a V position and placing under nose

22. Maurice, 23. Endora loses her powers 24. Deacon Jones, 25. Bernie Kopell, 26. Clients, 27. Genius, 28. Dr. Bombay, 29. Ankle, 30. She fades, 31. She was an aging witch and her powers were dwindling,

32. Earthbound, 33. usually Serena, 34. Harriet, 35. Serena,

36. Howard, 37. Margaret, 38. Louise Sorel, 39. Bar, 40. usually Dobbin, 41. The Witch Doctor, 42. Sidney, 43. Hopkins Realty,

44. 555-2134, 555-7328, or 555-2368, 45. 555-6059, 46. 4R6 558,

47. Jean Pierre, 48. Sammy, 49. Yes, Episode #41, 50. Good for You!!!!

51. Madge, 52. "I'll Blow You A Kiss In The Wind," 53. January 23, 1963, 54. Sorrento's Restaurant, 55. Hepzibah, 56. Screen Gems,

57. Sol Saks, 58. Stew, 59. Darrin The Bold, 60. 32nd Floor, 61. Grover,

62. International Building, 63. Chevrolet or Quaker Oats, 64. Ticheba; 65. Nose

His or Hers:

Hers
Hers
Hers
Neither, Hepzibah is the High Priestess over witchdom.
Hers
Hers

His
Hers
Neither
Neither
Neither
Neither
Hers
Neither
Neither

Answers to the Six Neither from His or Hers Section:

1. Betty, Darrin's secretary
2. Dr. Bombay, Sam's family physician
3. Jon Tate, Larry and Louise Tate's son
4. Gladys Kravitz, next door neighbor
5. Sidney Kravitz, Gladys' nephew
6. The Apothecary, Sam's pharmacist

Easy Multiple Choice:

1. D 2. B; 3. B; 4. D; 5. D ; 6. B; 7. B&C; 8. A; 9. B; 10. D; 11. D; 12. A; 13. B; 14. C ; 15. D; 16. B ; 17. C ; 18. C 19. A; 20.A 21.B.; 22. A. Mother Goose; 23. B. Mario's; 24. A. Sick Headache; 25. A. eight seasons

Tabitha Comedy Trivia answers:

1.Second pilot aired on November 12, 1977, 2. August 25, 1978, 3. Bewitched, 4. ABC, 5. Lisa Hartman, 6. David Ankrum, 7. Tabitha worked as a production assistant *on The Paul Thurston Show*, a Los Angeles television program, 8.Aunt Minerva, 9. She was too young at the time, Bewitched had ended only five years earlier. The producers wanted a twenty-something Tabitha. 10. Los Angeles, California, 11. Paul Thurston, 12. By the use of witchcraft, 13. Lisa Hartman 14. Tabitha's boss, 15. one 16. William Asher 17. Liberty Williams, 18. Convertible Volkswagen, 19. Yellow

I Dream of Jeannie Déjà vu Answers:

1. NBC, Genie, Jeannie; 2. Nelson (eventually she convinced Tony to marry her, though the beginning years Jeannie was last nameless); 3. A. Get him to marry her; 4. A. True; 5. C. Psychiatrist at Captain Nelson's base; 6. B. Jeannie, bien sur (French for of course, not her actual name)

B. 29 days; 7. C. The Ordeal by Fire Warlock Test; 8. A. Endora; 9. B. 400 years; 10. A. 10,000 spell checkup and overhaul.

Answers to Tabitha Stephens Trivia:

1.A. January 13, 1966; 2. C. Perkins; 3. C. Endora; 4. C. Gazelle; 5. C. Erin and Diane Murphy; 6. A. Erin Murphy; 7. Dr. Koblin; 8. A. Chocolate pudding; 9. a. The Moment of Truth; 10. B. Uncle Arthur

Answers to "I Don't Want to Be a Toad": Delightful Day Nursery School, Amy, toad, butterfly, lost, close

Romance Taking Flight, Samantha and Darrin Answers:

1. B. going through a revolving door; 2. A. New York City; 3. B. a pink wool dress; 4. C. their first quarrel; 5.B. a watch; 6. C. James and Susan; 7. A. Sorrento's Restaurant; 8. C. Walking through a Revolving Door; 9. B. Sheila; 10. A. She tells Samantha to dress casually to a dinner party; 12. A. It disappears; 12. C. Clara

Witches and Warlocks are my Favorite Things Trivia Answers:

1. B. Bertha; 2. B. The Centennial Convocation of the Witches of the World; 3.A. High Priestess Hepzibah; 4. C. Good Luck; 5. A. A Witch-O-Gram; 6. A. Rollo, Endora; 7. A. Panda; 8. B. Hong Kong; 9. Sir Walter Raleigh

Extreme Home Makeover Answers:

1. B. All In The Family; 2. A. It Keeps appearing and disappearing; 3. A. New Plumbing; 4. B. 1164 Morning Glory Circle; 5. B. Westport, Conneticut; 6. B. Hopkins Realty; 7. A. Blue; 8. B. Orange and green tiles; 9. C. Pink; 10. B. Yellow; 11. A. Darrin thinks Samantha has conjured up synthetic grass in the front yard; 12. C. A new home is a nice place to live.

CHAPTER 8

In Witch Conclusion

A little about Me:

A self-described *Bewitched* expert by the time I was twelve, I have seen every *Bewitched* episode, and have memorized quite a few of them. I am constantly surprised when I do run across a *Bewitched* show that I haven't seen as much. It is also fun to share those memories and experiences with my husband and children. Recently, my daughter Lauren said, "Mom, you've seen this episode a lot before." Sometimes, the less viewed ones, the ones I didn't see on network television growing up, seem fresh and new to me. I responded to my ten year old by saying, "I think you've actually seen this one more than me." It was obvious after all, she had told me the entire plot and the ending.

When I was a child, I often wrote and scripted *Bewitched* plays and would produce the plays in my backyard where I frequently cast myself as Samantha. My neighborhood friend, Rosalie, often would be Serena. As her mom Rachel recently recounted, "Rose used to come home pouting, saying in disgust,('why does Gina always have to be Samantha!')" Though at the time I had no idea she was upset, I reasoned that since I was directing, writing, and producing the plays, I might as well be my hero, Samantha. I also reasoned that Rosalie had dark hair like Serena, and I thought it was a compliment.

I started researching for *The Magic of Bewitched Trivia and More* when I was in junior high school, spending afternoons looking through vintage magazine articles at the Fresno State Library. In high school, while visiting my dad and grandparents in the summers, I would expand upon my information by going to the local San Francisco public libraries and locating articles about Elizabeth Montgomery, and *Bewitched* on microfiche. By college, I was compiling all of my years of research, writing, revising, and placing my work on disks. At this time, I started to freelance and consulting work for Nick at Nite, and Columbia Pictures. I also was fervently trying to market my book by sending countless proposals to publishing houses.

My life these days is a lot like Samantha Stephens. I am a suburban housewife, who is also an author, small business owner, and part time teacher. I juggle family responsibilities like laundry, bill paying, baking lasagna for dinner, cleaning the house (boy I wish I had one of the those self running-cleaning vacuums like Samantha.) with special time with my husband, and children. There is never enough time in the day to accomplish all that needs to be done. There are dance competitions, basketball season, cross country time, cheer, and choir, just to name a few activities that the children are involved with. There are lunches to make and clothes to iron. There are book signings and parties on the weekends. There are out of town trips on the holidays. I sure wish I had magical powers, they would sure come in handy!

Now that I am in my thirties, the *Bewitched* television series and other nostalgic television shows, such as *I Dream of Jeannie*, have become driving forces in my life. In 1991, I started The Magic of *Bewitched* Fan Club as well as the accompanying Morning Glory Gazette Newsletter. I have spoken with fans from all over the world who love *Bewitched* too! In 1994, I assisted Columbia House Video Library compiling twenty *Bewitched* videotapes. I named and grouped the videos according to themes and what I thought other *Bewitched* fans would enjoy. Some of my video titles include, "Witch Diseases", "Twitch or Treat", and "Serena". Columbia House Video Library only wanted to produce the Dick York years, so missing from my experience was the ability to name and theme the Dick Sargent Episodes. On a side note, I am anxious to see Dick Sargent *Bewitched* episodes produced onto DVD, it is still not yet a reality. In the summer of 1995, *Nick at Nite* Collectors Edition Magazine asked me to be a consultant for some sections of their magazine that involved *Bewitched* and *I Dream of Jeannie*. That summer, Barnes and Noble hosted a Bewitched trivia and costume contest with myself as the moderator. It was so exciting to see so many age groups represented at the trivia night wearing *Bewitched* tee-shirts and doing the witches honor sign. Since that first Barnes and Noble event, we have had signings in Walnut Creek, San Francisco, Las Vegas, Hawaii, Clovis, Glendale, and San Jose-just to name a few. We have also arranged Bewitching events such as PJ's, Popcorn, and Pop culture in September of 2005 at Sierra Vista Mall in Clovis, California. A select group of girls from Clovis Academy of Dance and Gymnastics, danced to the *Bewitched* theme and the theme song from the Rock Hudson and Doris Day Movie, *Pillow Talk*. 150 people came to the event and individuals who got *Bewitched* trivia questions correct, received *Bewitched* Bucks which recipients later redeeming them for memorabilia. At that magical event, I met Greg Madel and David Mandel-Bloch's (the twins who played Adam) half sister and a stage hand that used to work on the *Bewitched* set.

The Magic of Bewitched: Trivia and *The Magic of Bewitched Trivia and More* books have been labors of love. Quite like having Lucas and Lauren, now three and ten years old respectively, and my stepdaughter Makenna who is sixteen. Right before completion of the second book, *The Magic of Bewitched Trivia*, my daughter Lauren reminded me, "Now, don't forget to add stuff about Pandora Spocks." She, like me, has always been fascinated with Elizabeth Montgomery's sense of humor. To credit her portrayal of Serena with the name Pandora Spocks is hysterical! And we always thought Paul Lynde/Uncle Arthur was the jokester. I have to remind myself that the entire family has been on this journey together-from book signings to television crews filming our lives, to just watching *Bewitched* as a family.

From my family to yours, thank you for making *The Magic of Bewitched Trivia* book a part of your day. To the fans that make this journey ever meaningful, merci beaucoup, mucas gracias!

Bewitched Fans from all over the globe in front of the *Bewitched* House Façade. Photo provided by David Lawrence Meyers.

Want More Information on *Bewitched*?

Trivia Tidbit: *Bewitched*, Season 5 will come out on DVD July of 2007

A website devoted to selling *Bewitched* merchandise and the ability to contact the author for speaking engagements and booking events.
www.magicofbewitched.com

The Magic of *Bewitched* Fan Club and Newsletter
P.O. Box 26734
Fresno, CA 93729
Contact: gina@magicofbewitched.com

David Meyers has been a graphic designer for twenty years. He produces award-winning graphic design nationally as well as internationally. His most recent freelance account is with the country western singer Kenny Chesney's management group. Contact David for any graphic needs. d@magicofbewitched.com

Bewitched Websites:
Beguiling and Bewitching episode from the television show Fanatical features Gina Meyers (author) and Mark Simpson (Bewitched Collector) in an half an hour format showing off their Bewitched collections' and Gina's cooking talents as well as entertaining skills (from the Bewitched Bash put on for charity, shown in the episode).
www.fanatical.tv

Bewitched Collectibles (see Mark R. Simpson's' expansive Bewitched collection and hear about the latest Bewitched news.)
Mark Simpson, the "*Bewitched* Collector" and Gina Meyers at the Ranch, photo courtesy of David Lawrence Meyers, July 2005)
http://bewitchedcollector.tripod.com

Ross N. Allison is known as the Bewitched artist, he has *Bewitched* inspired art for sale including magnets, postcards, and original limited edition prints.
http://bewitchedartist.tripod.com

The first Bewitched website. Features special articles on *Bewitched*, interviews wit the stars from Bewitched, books inspired from Bewitched, and one of a kind photographs.
www.bewitched.net

Great discussion board with current up to date information on all of the Bewitched happenings.
www.harpiesbizarre.com

Causes Worth Supporting

Bewitching Fact:

Dick York and his wife Joey devoted their time to the homeless.

Elizabeth Montgomery supported her friend Dick Sargent by going with him to Gay Pride rallies.

When Elizabeth Montgomery was married to William Asher, she and her husband were involved in many worthwhile causes including UNICEF.

Samantha, though a fictional character, was heavily involved in social causes and reform. This may be a partial explanation for fans loving her so much and why she was so endearing to us. Samantha twitched for many causes including supporting a city councilman, fighting City Hall in order to save a park, and collecting money for UNICEF. Samantha combated prejudice in "Sisters at Heart", "Trick or Treat", as well as "Samantha's Thanksgiving to Remember".

One of my first videos that I did for Columbia House was entitled, "Jealousy". Another title was, "Money Isn't Everything". The word jealousy has the word lousy in it and jealousy in my book is one of the worst human emotions. It evokes hate and fear. Where jealousy exits, so too does a power struggle on a multitude of levels. So too does envy and selfish ambition. *Bewitched* was a love story, but it also was a vehicle for people who didn't have a voice to be heard. In "Witches Are People Too", Mr. Brinkman wants to capitalize on the stereotypical witch, an old ugly crone and use it in his advertising campaign. Samantha convinces her husband Darrin that if he is married to one, then he should use his advertising savvy to steer Mr. Brinkman into a more flattering image of who witches really are. I'm not a real witch, but I have been persecuted, rejected, belittled, demeaned, and mistreated for a number of reasons. Too short, too pretty, too smart, too assertive, too poor, too rich, too Sicilian, too Italian, too etc. Prejudice still exists and unwritten "rules" still prevail. How is one expected to behave in a contemporary society in which archaic rules and principles exist. It is a constant battle between ones' own belief system, and a system which imposes its' restrictions on the human race. We only have one life to live and if we can truly get our point across in a compassionate way, I believe this is essential to getting along with others. No one said that navigating in this world is an easy one, however, Samantha Stephens was the true epitome of a caring, compassionate witch. There are many people in this world who have daily struggles emotionally, physically, and mentally. Let us remember that Bewitched wasn't just a romantic comedy, it fostered much more. Take the time to support a cause close to your heart. Down below is just one example of an opportunity to share your love.

NAMI is the National Alliance on Mental Illness, it is the largest grassroots mental health organization dedicated to improving the lives of persons living with mental disorders and their families. People with mental illness are from all walks of life, all socioeconomic classes, and all races. Mental illness does not discriminate.
NAMI National
2107 Wilson Blvd. Suite 300
Arlington, VA 22201
info@nami.org
www.nami.org
Helpline: 800-950-NAMI

About the Author

Beguiling and Bewitching are two words that describe how **Gina Meyers** feels about the magical 1960's sitcom Bewitched, that is still enormously popular on DVD and in syndication today. Gina Meyers is a *Bewitched* expert who was recently featured on the popular Canadian television series Fanatical! Her trivia tibits have been utilized in magazines and on television. Mrs. Meyers has logged countless hours in the 1980's watching Bewitched in reruns and now as a wife and mother still loving the show. Gina has been a Bewitched consultant for Nick at Nite as well as for Columbia House Video Library. She has been fortunate to have gone on a booksigning tour with Louise Tate #2, Kasey Rogers. This is Gina's second trivia book. Her first, *The Magic of Bewitched Trivia and More* has sold over 2,000 copies. Simply Magical!!!

978-0-595-44744-2
0-595-44744-9